A
BIBLIOGRAPHY
OF
SLAVIC MYTHOLOGY

A
BIBLIOGRAPHY
OF
SLAVIC MYTHOLOGY

by

Mark Kulikowski

Slavica Publishers, Inc.

Slavica publishes a wide variety of books and journals dealing with the peoples, languages, literatures, history, folklore, and culture of the peoples of Eastern Europe and the USSR. For a complete catalog with prices and ordering information, please write to:

Slavica Publishers, Inc.
P.O. Box 14388
Columbus, Ohio 43214
USA

ISBN: 0-89357-203-9

Text set by Randy Bowlus, at the East European Composition Center, supported by the Department of Slavic Languages and Literatures and the Center for Russian and East European Studies at UCLA.

Printed in the United States of America.

TABLE OF CONTENTS

INTRODUCTION

Like the early history of the Slavs (9th–12th centuries A.D.), Slavic mythology has always presented a challenge to the scholar. Few written documents on this topic exist, and as a result, scholars have been obliged to draw material from other fields—art, folklore, archeology—to support their ideas. Even with this information, the evaluation of early Slavic belief is a very difficult task.

Owing to the difficulties involved, most histories scarcely treat Slavic belief before conversion to Christianity. Clearly, conversion is an important historical event, but it is incorrect to assume that the attitudes and beliefs of pre-Christian Slavdom were rapidly discarded. Many of the attitudes and beliefs which characterized pre-Christian Slavic culture remained in force, and, although altered to meet the demands of Christianity, played a role in the development of Slavic civilization.

The study of Slavic pagan belief began as early as the seventeenth century. These early studies were often brief, general accounts, loosely based on medieval written sources and folklore. Investigations of this sort continued down to, and throughout the eighteenth century. Despite the growing interest shown in this topic, much of the work proved to be unsystematic in approach and, in some cases, based on unreliable information.[1]

It was not until the second half of the nineteenth century that a systematic study of Slavic pagan belief began. During this period a number of relevant medieval texts were edited and published. Archeological discoveries in Slavic areas of Europe also added important details. The information from these and other sources expanded and clarified much of what was known about early Slavic history and pagan beliefs. Scholars like Alexander Brueckner dealt with questions on a far more sophisticated level than had their predecessors. Scholarly interest grew appreciably during this period. By the end of the century, while the quantity of information on this topic had grown only moderately, it was clear that many of the earlier views of ancient Slavic belief required modification.

By the turn of the century a Czech scholar, Lubor Niederle, completed his investigation of ancient Slavic culture. The result of this investigation was his massive *Slovanské starožitnosti* (Slavic antiquities). Niederle's analysis of ancient Slavic religion was based on the critical use of medieval sources, folklore, and recent archeological discoveries. To this body of information, Niederle brought a new interpretation. He sought to show how the beliefs of the ancient Slavs evolved from their contact with nature.[2] Niederle saw ancient Slavic belief as a series of stages, progressing from the personification of natural phenomenon to the creation of gods.[3] He supported his thesis with an encyclopedic knowledge of the Slavic and Classical past. It was through his efforts that the scientific study of Slavic antiquities was established.

The twentieth century has seen the study of ancient Slavic belief conducted in a variety of ways. The multiplicity of approaches indicates the variety of data available to the scholar. For example, S. A. Tokarev employed ethnographic information,[4] while V. V. Ivanov and V. N. Toporov[5] have used linguistic, semiotic, and folklore analyses. Large-scale studies of Slavic belief have also been completed. These include H. Łowmiański's *Religia Słowian i jej upadek* (The Religion of the Slavs and its fall),[6] and B. A. Rybakov's *Iazychestvo drevnikh slavian* (The Paganism of the ancient Slavs).[7] As a result of such efforts, scholars can look forward to an increased understanding of this period of Slavic history.

Despite the progress being made in the field, it would appear that there has been little communication among scholars investigating this subject. Articles and books on Slavic pagan religion cite the same primary sources, but rarely the same secondary sources. It seems that a great deal of useful information on the subject is being missed. If we are to come to a new assessment of this topic, a collected body of research is essential. It was with this in mind that I began compiling this bibliography. Its principal purpose is to fill a gap in our knowledge and aid in the further investigation of the field.

The scope of the bibliography is all written materials (books, dissertations, pamphlets, articles, and selections) from the earliest times up to and including 1981, published in all Slavic and major Western languages. A small number of items from 1982 have also been included, but full coverage for that year is not claimed. On the whole, I have not included discussions of Slavic mythology which appeared in general history texts, general encyclopedias, dictionaries, and newspapers. A small number of exceptions were made for items of particular significance.

The topics covered by this bibliography include: the pantheon of the gods, their priests, temples, cult places, and so on. Items relating to the coversion of the Slavs were included only if they dealt substantially with some aspect of Slavic mythology. Lesser gods and supernatural beings, witchcraft, ancestor worship, funerary pratices, and the remnants of mythology in Slavic folklore and customs, while important to our overall understanding, are not included here.[8] I have limited the primary source section to those books which are considered the major sources for the subject.

While I have aimed at comprehensive coverage of the topics, there is undoubtedly material I have missed. I would greatly appreciate learning of any omissions or errors I have made. I have seen virtually all but a handful of the items listed here. In those cases where I was unable to personally examine the material, I have relied on information provided by professional researchers.

Individual entries have been arranged in the following manner: author, title, place of publication, publisher, pagination, series (if any), Library of

Congress call number, library locations, and review (if applicable). In the case of entries in Slavic languages, a translation of the title follows the body of the entry. A slightly modified version of this format has been employed for articles and selections. Reviews, where applicable, have been limited to one per entry. I have not tried to be selective in citing reviews, other than to limit the reviews to those appearing in scholarly journals. Anonymous entries have been listed alphabetically under the title, or under the author's initials, when known.

Periodicals issued by an institution are normally listed under that institution. For example, *Zhurnal Ministerstva Narodnogo Prosveshcheniia* will be cited as follows: Russia. Ministerstvo Narodnogo Prosveshcheniia. *Zhurnal.*

I have followed the Library of Congress transliteration system, using diacritical marks when needed, except in the cases where the original material was in Cyrillic. Umlauts have been extended, i.e. ä = ae, etc.

This bibliography is intended primarily for an American audience. The list of library locations reflects this intention. Primarily American and Canadian libraries are listed. I have based my list of library locations on the entries found in the *National Union Catalogue of Pre–1956 Imprints, National Union/Library of Congress Catalogue, Cyrillic Union Catalogue, Slavic Cyrillic Union Catalogue,* and the *New York Public Library Slavonic Collection Catalogue,* among others. In a number of cases, material cited is not reported as existing in American or Canadian libraries. In these cases I have tried to supply a list of libraries in Great Britain, France, the Federal Republic of Germany, the German Democratic Republic and the USSR which report holding this material. There are some entries for which I was unable to ascertian any library holdings. These entries have been made as complete as possible, and are listed for the record.

In addition to the entries, I have included a list of abbreviations, a list of library symbols and addresses, and separate author, title, and subject indexes. Also included is a list of periodicals/serials listed. Review journals are included. The list contains bibliographic information on the periodicals (title, place of publication, date(s) of publication, Library of Congress call number, library locations). I have limited the list of library locations to those libraries which report having a complete or near complete run of the periodical/serial cited. It is hoped that this information will facilitate the scholar's location of the material.[9]

I would like to thank a number of individuals and institutions that provided advice and support for this project. My special thanks to Professors Sidney Harcave, Alton Donnelly, and Thadd Hall of the History Department, State University of New York at Binghamton for their advice and encouragement. My thanks also to Professor Charles Gribble, editor of Slavica Publishers for his advice and patience. The efforts of the Interlibrary Loan staffs of the State University of New York at Binghamton and State

University of New York, College at Oswego in acquiring various items for me are greatly appreciated. Special acknowledgment is in order for June Pachuta Farris, Harold Leich, Laurence Miller, and the staff of the Slavic and East European Division, Library, University of Illinois, Champaign-Urbana, who gave sound advice and unraveled a number of difficult bibliographic problems. My thanks to the staff of the Library of Congress, the staff of the Olin Library, Cornell University, the director and staff of the Slavonic Division, New York Public Library, and the staffs of the Lenin Library (Moscow), the State Public Historical Library (Moscow), and the Library of the Academy of Sciences of the USSR (Leningrad) for their help. Lastly, I would like to thank the Office of International Programs, State University of New York for giving me the opportunity to do research in the Soviet Union in 1979–1980, and the Russian and East European Center, University of Illinois, Champaign-Urbana, for selecting me to participate in a number of Summer Research Laboratories at the University.

NOTES

1. Tokarev, Sergei A. "Niederle's views on the religious beliefs of the ancient Slavs in the light of the latest research," *Ethnologia Slavica*, 1 (1969) p. 47, Znayenko, Myroslava T. *The gods of the ancient Slavs. Tatishchev and the beginnings of Slavic mythology* (Columbus: Slavica, 1980), pp. 97–102.

2. Tokarev, pp. 51, 54–55.

3. Tokarev, pp. 56–59.

4. Tokarev, Sergei A. *Religioznye verovaniia vostochnoslavianskikh narodov XIX – nachala XX veka* (Moscow–Leningrad, 1957).

5. Ivanov, V. V. & Toporov, V. N. *Issledovaniia v oblasti slavianskikh drevnostei* (Moscow: Nauka, 1974). Also their *Slavianskie iazykovye modeliruiushchie semioticheskie sistemy: drevnii period* (Moscow: Nauka, 1965).

6. Łowmiański, Henryk. *Religia Słowian i jej upadek* (Warsaw: Państwowe Wydawnictwo Naukowe, 1979).

7. Rybakov, B. A. *Iazychestvo drevnikh slavian* (Moscow: Nauka, 1981).

8. For further information on these topics, see: Sumtsov, N. F. "Kolduny, vied'my i upyri. (Bibliograficheskii ukazatel')," Khar'kov. Universytet. Istoriko-filologicheskoe obshchestvo. *Sbornik*, 3 (1891) pp. 229–278. Also issued as a pamphlet. Pomerantseva, E. V. *Mifologicheskie personazhi v russkom fol'klore* (Moscow, 1975), Kotliarevskii, A. A. *O pogrebal'nykh obychaiakh iazycheskikh slavian* (Moscow, 1868), Veletskaia, N. N. *Iazycheskaia simvolika slavianskikh arkhaicheskikh ritualov* (Moscow, 1978), Zelenin, D. K. *Russische (ostslavische) Volkskunde* (Berlin, 1927), Zguta, R. *Russian minstrels: the history of the Skomorokhi)* (Philadelphia, 1979).

9. For those interested in biographical information on some of the authors in this bibliography, see: *Slavianovedenie v dorevoliutsionnoi Rossii. Biobibliograficheskii slovar'* (Moscow, 1979), *Istoriki-slavisty SSSR. Biobibliograficheskii slovar'-spravochnik* (Moscow, 1981), Bulakhau, M. N. *Vostochnoslavianskie iazykovedy: bibliograficheskii slovar'* (Minsk, 1976–78), *Polski słownik biograficzny* (Krakow, 1935–).

ABBREVIATIONS

Ab.	Abteilung
ANSSSR	Akademiia nauk SSSR
Auf.	Auflage
BAN	Bulgarska akademiia na naukite
Bd.	Band
ch.	chast'
chap.	chapter
comp.	compiler
cz.	część
ed.	editor
fasc.	fascicle
Gos.	Gosudarstvennoe
H.	heft
inst.	institut
izd., izd-vo	izdatel'stvo
kn.	kniga
knj.	knjiga
lit.	litografiia
N.F.	Neue Folge
n.p.	no place of publication
N.S.	Nova serija
Nakl., Nakł	Nakladatel', nakładca
no.	number
otd.	otdel
pseud.	pseudonym
Sv.	svazek
t.	tom, tome
Tip.	tipografiia
Tov., T-va	tovarishchestvo
Univ., un-ta	universitet
v.	volume
vyp.	vypusk
Wydawn.	wydawnictwo
z.	zeszyt

LIST OF LIBRARY SYMBOLS

A   Bibliothèque inter-universitaire d'Aix-Marseille. Section
           Droit-Lettres. Avenue Robert-Schumann, 13606 —
           Aix-en-Provence, France

AAP   Ralph Brown Draughton Library, Auburn University,
           Auburn, Alabama 36830

AbU   University College of Wales Library, Absersystwyth, Car-
           diganshire, Great Britain

AD   Union Centrale des Arts Décoratifs, Bibliothèque, Palais
           du Louvre, 107, rue de Rivoli, 75001 — Paris, France

AkU   Elmer E. Rasmuson Library, University of Alaska, Fair-
           banks, Alaska 99701

ANSSSR-
INION   Institut nauchnoi informatsii po obshchestvennym naukam
           Akademii nauk SSSR, ul. Krasikov, 28-45, Moskva,
           USSR

AU   Amelia Gayle Gorgas Library, Box S, University of Ala-
           bama, University, Alabama 35486

AU   University of Aberdeen Library, King's College, Aberdeen,
           Great Britain

AzTeS   Library, Arizona State University, Tempe, Arizona 85281

AzU   University of Arizona Library, Tucson, Arizona 85721

BAN   Biblioteka Akademii nauk SSSR. Birzhevaia liniia 1,
           119164 Leningrad V-164, USSR

BANBelo   Fundamental'naia biblioteka Akademii nauk Belorusskoi
           SSR imeni Iakuba Kolosa. Leninskii pr. 66, Minsk,
           USSR

BANEst   Nauchnaia biblioteka Akademii nauk Estonskoi SSR. ul.
           Lenina, 10, Tallin, USSR

BANLit   Tsentral'naia biblioteka Akademii nauk Litovskoi SSR. ul.
           Pozhelos 2/8, Vil'nius, USSR

BANUkr   Tsentral'naia nauchnaia biblioteka Akademii nauk USSR,
           Vladimirskaia 62, Kiev, USSR

BBeloSSR   Gosudarstvennaia biblioteka BSSR imeni V.I. Lenina, ul.
           Krasnoarmeiskaia 9, Minsk, USSR

BLitSSR   Gosudarstvennaia respublikanskaia biblioteka Litovskoi
           SSR, pr. Lenina 51, Vil'nius, USSR

BlU   The Queen's University of Belfast Library, Belfast, BT7
           1NN Great Britain

BM   The British Library, Great Russell Street, London, WC1B
           3DG Great Britain

BN	Bibliothèque Nationale. 58, rue Richelieu, 75084 — Paris CEDEX 02 France
BP	Birmingham Public Libraries, Central Library, Ratcliff Pl., Birmingham 1, Great Britain
BrP	Bristol Public Libraries, Central Library, College Green, Bristol 1, Great Britain
BSarU	Nauchnaia Biblioteka Saratovskogo Universiteta imeni Chernyshevskogo. Universitetskaia ul. 42, Saratov, USSR
BU	University of Birmingham Library, P.O. Box 363, Edgbaston, Birmingham 15, Great Britain
Bx	Bibliothèque inter-universitaire de Bordeaux. Section Centrale. Avenue des Arts, Domaine Universitaire, 33405 — Talence, France
C	California State Library, 914 Capitol Mall, P.O. Box 2037, Sacramento, California 95809
C	University Library, University of Cambridge, Burrell's Walk, Cambridge, Great Britain
CaAEU	University Libraries, University of Alberta, Edmonton, Alberta, T6G 2J8 Canada
CaBVa	Vancouver Public Library, 750 Burrard Street, Vancouver, British Columbia, V6Z 1X5 Canada
CaBVaU	University of British Columbia Library, 2075 Westbrook Pl., Vancouver, British Columbia, V6T 1W5 Canada
CaBViV	McPherson Library, University of Victoria, P.O. Box 1800, Victoria, British Columbia, V8W 2Y3 Canada
CaMWU	Elizabeth Dafoe Library, University of Manitoba, Winnipeg, Manitoba, R3T 2N2 Canada
CAN	School of Anatomy, University of Cambridge, Cambridge, Great Britain
CaNBFU	Harriet Irving Library, P.O. Box 7500, University of New Brunswick, Fredericton, New Brunswick, E3B 5H5 Canada
CaOKQ	Douglas Library, Queen's University, Kingston, Ontario, K7L 5L4 Canada
CaOOCC	Murdoch Maxwell MacOdrum Library, Carleton University, Colonel By Drive, Ottawa, Ontario, K1S 5B6 Canada
CaOONM	National Museums of Canada Library, 2086 Walkley Rd., Ottawa, Ontario K1A 0M8 Canada
CaOOU	Morisset Library, University of Ottawa, 65 Hastey, Ottawa, Ontario K1N 6N5 Canada

CaOTP	Toronto Public Library, 40 Orchard View Blvd., Toronto, Ontario M4R 1B9 Canada
CaOTRM	Royal Ontario Museum Library, 100 Queen's Park, Toronto, M5S 2C6 Canada
CaOTU	University Library, University of Toronto, Toronto, Ontario M5S 1A5 Canada
CaOTY	Leslie Frost Library, York University, 2275 Bayview Ave., Toronto, Ontario M4N 3M6 Canada
CaOWA	Leddy Library, University of Windsor, Windsor, Ontario N9B 3P4 Canada
CaOWtU	Library, University of Waterloo, Waterloo, Ontario N2L 3G1 Canada
CaQMM	McGill University Libraries, 3459 McTavish St., Montreal, Quebec H3A 1Y1 Canada
CaQMU	University of Montreal Libraries, Box 6128, Montreal, Quebec H3C 3J7 Canada
CaSSU	University of Saskatchewan Library, Saskatoon, Saskatchewan S7N OWW Canada
CCC	Claremont Colleges Libraries, Ninth & Dartmouth Sts, Claremont, California 91711
CH	Haddon Library, Faculty of Archaeology and Anthropology, University of Cambridge, Downing St., Cambridge, Great Britain
CL	Los Angeles Public Library, 630 W. Fifth Street, Los Angeles, California 90071
CLSU	Edward L. Doheny Memorial Library, University of Southern California, University Park, Los Angeles, California 90007
CLU	University Library, University of California at Los Angeles, 405 Hilgard Ave., Los Angeles, California 90024
CNoS	Delmar T. Oviatt & South Libraries, California State University, Northridge, 18111 Nordhoff St., Northridge, California 91330
CoDB	Bibliographic Center for Research, Rocky Mountain Region Inc., 245 Columbine, Suite 212, Denver, Colorado 80206
CoFS	William E. Morgan Library, Colorado State University, Fort Collins, Colorado 80523
CoG	Arthur Lakes Library, Colorado School of Mines, Golden, Colorado 80401
CoU	University Libraries, University of Colorado at Boulder, M450, Boulder, Colorado 80309
CSmH	Huntington Library, 1151 Oxford Rd., San Marino, California 91108

CSt	University & Coordinate Libraries, Stanford University, Stanford, California 94305
CSt-H	Library, Hoover Institution on War, Revolution and Peace, Stanford, California 94305
CtU	Library, University of Connecticut, Storrs, Connecticut 06268
CtW	Olin Memorial Library, Wesleyan University, Middletown, Connecticut 06457
CtY	Yale University Library, 120 High Street, Box 1603A, Yale Station, New Haven, Connecticut 06520
CtY-D	Library, Divinity School, Yale University, 409 Prospect Street, New Haven, Connecticut 06510
CU	University Library, University of California, Berkeley. Berkeley, California 94720
CU-Riv	University Library, University of California, Riverside, 4045 Canyon Crest Drive, P.O. Box 5900, Riverside, California 92507
CU-S	University Libraries, University of California, San Diego. La Jolla, California 92093
CU-SB	Library, Univeristy of California, Santa Barbara. Santa Barbara, California 93106
CU-SC	Library, University of California, Santa Cruz. Santa Cruz, California 95064
DAU	Battelle-Tompkins Memorial Library, American University, Massachusetts & Nebraska Aves., NW, Washington, D.C. 20016
DCU	John K. Mullen of Denver Memorial Library, Catholic University of America, 620 Michigan Ave., NE, Washington, D.C. 20064
DDO	Dumbarton Oaks Research Library of Harvard University, Washington, D.C. 20007
DeU	Hugh M. Morris Library, University of Delaware, Newark, Delaware 19711
DGW	George Washington University Library, 2130 H St., NW, Washington, D.C. 20052
DLC	Library of Congress, 10 First St., SE, Washington, D.C. 20540
DLC-P4	Priority 4 Collection, Library of Congress, 10 First St., SE, Washington, D.C. 20540
DS	Library, U.S. Department of State, 22nd & C Sts., NW, Washington, D.C. 20520
DSI	Smithsonian Institution Library, Constitution Ave. & 10th St., NW, Washington, D.C. 20560

EMA	National Museum of Antiquities of Scotland, Edinburgh 2, Great Britain
EU	University of Edinburgh Library, George Square, Edinburgh, EH8 9LJ Great Britain
FJ	Haydon Burns Library, Jacksonville Public Library System, 122 N. Ocean St., Jacksonville, Florida 32202
FM	Miami-Dade Public Library System, 1 Biscayne Blvd., Miami, Florida 33132
FMU	Otto G. Richter Library, University of Miami, Memorial Drive, P.O. Box 248214, Coral Gables, Florida 33124
FTaSU	Robert Manning Strozier Library, Florida State University, Tallahassee, Florida 32306
FU	University of Florida Libraries, University of Florida, Gainesville, Florida 32611
GASU	William Russell Pullen Library, George State University, 100 Decatur St., SE, Atlanta, Georgia 30303
GAT	Price Gilbert Memorial Library, Georgia Institute of Technology, Atlanta, Georgia 30332
GBIL	Vsesoiuznaia Gosudarstvennaia Biblioteka Inostrannoi Literatury, Ul'ianovskaia ul. 1, Moskva, USSR
GEU	Library, Emory University, Atlanta, Georgia 30322
GLB	Gotha Landesbibliothek, Schloss Friedenstein, Gotha, German Democratic Republic
GPIB	Gosudarstvennaia Publichnaia Istoricheskaia Biblioteka RSFSR, ul. Bogdana Khmel'nitskogo, Starosadskii per. 9, 101839 Moskva, USSR
GU	Library, University of Georgia, Athens, Georgia 30602
GU	Glasgow University Library, Glasgow W2, Great Britain
I	Institut de France, Bibliothèque, 23, Quai Conti, 75270 — Paris CEDEX 06 France
IaAS	Iowa State University Library, Ames, Iowa 50011
IaU	University of Iowa Libraries, University of Iowa, Iowa City, Iowa 52242
IC	Institut catholique de France, Bibliothèque, 21, rue d'Assas, 75270 — Paris CEDEX 06 France
ICF	Library, Field Museum of Natural History, Roosevelt Rd. & Lake Shore Dr., Chicago, Illinois 60605
ICIU	Library, University of Illinois at Chicago Circle, 801 South Morgan St., P.O. Box 8198, Chicago, Ilinois 60680
ICJ	John Crerar Library, 35 W. 33rd St., Chicago, Illinois 60616
ICMcC	McGaw Memorial Library, McCormick Theological Seminary, 1100 E. 55th St., Chicago, Illinois 60615

ICN	The Newberry Library, 60 W. Walton St., Chicago, Illinois 60610
ICRL	Center for Research Libraries, 5721 Cottage Grove Ave., Chicago, Illinois 60637
ICU	Joseph Regenstein Library, University of Chicago, 1100 E. 57th St., Chicago, Illinois 60637
IEdS	Library, Southern Illinois University, Edwardsville Campus, Edwardsville, Illinois 62025
IEG	Library, Garrett-Evangelical Theological Seminary, 2121 Sheridan Rd., Evnston, Illinois 60201
IEN	Library, Northwestern University, 1935 Sheridan Rd., Evanston, Illinois 60201
InLP	Purdue University Libraries, Stewart Center, West Lafayette, Indiana 47907
InNd	University Library, University of Notre Dame, Notre Dame, Indiana 46556
InU	University Libraries, Indiana University, Tenth St. & Jordan Ave., Bloomington, Indiana 47401
IU	Library, University of Illinois, 1408 W. Gregory, Urbana, Illinois 61801
JGH	Johann Gottfried Herder Institut, Bibliothek, Gisonenweg 5-7, 3550 Marburg/Lahn, Federal Repubilc of Germany
KAS	North Campus Library, Benedictine College, Second & Division, Atchinson, Kansas 66002
KEmT	William Allen White Library, 1200 Commercial Street, Emporia State Univrsity, Emporia, Kansas 66801
KharGU	Tsentral'naia nauchnaia biblioteka Khar'kovskogo Gosudarstvennogo Universiteta imeni A.M. Gor'kogo, Universitetskaia ul. 23, Khar'kov, USSR
KievGU	Gosudarstvennaia nauchnaia biblioteka Kievskogo Universiteta imeni T.G. Shevchenko, Vladimirskaia 58, Kiev, USSR
KMK	Farrell Library, Kansas State University, Manhattan & Anderson Sts., Manhattan, Kansas 66506
KU	Watson Memorial Library, University of Kansas, Lawrence, Kansas 66045
KyU	Margaret I. King Library, University of Kentucky, Lexington, Kentucky 40506
L	Bibliothèque inter-universitaire. Domaine universitaire Littéraire et Juridique, 59650 — Villeneuve-D'ASCQ, France

LAI	Royal Anthropological Institute of Great Britain & Ireland, 21 Bedford Sq., London WC1, Great Britain
LB	Library, Bedford College, University of London, Regent's Park, London NW1, Great Britain
LCA	Courtauld Institute of Art, Univrsity of London, 20 Portman Sq., London W1H 0BE Great Britain
LdP	Leeds Public Libraries, Central Library, Leeds 1, Great Britain
LdU	The Brotherton Library, University of Leeds, The University, Leeds LS2 9JT Great Britain
LE	British Library of Political & Economic Science, Houghton St., London WC2, Great Britain
LErm	Biblioteka Gosudarstvennogo Ermitazh, Leningrad, Dvortsovaia naberezhnaia, 34, USSR
LFL	The Folklore Society, c/o University College London, Gower St., London WC1, Great Britain
LGL	Geological Society of London, Burlington House, London W1, Great Britain
LGU	Nauchnaia Biblioteka imeni Gor'kogo Leningradskogo Gosudarstvennogo Universiteta imeni A.A. Zhdanova, Universitetskaia naberezhnaia, 7, Leningrad, USSR
LK	King's College, University of London, Strand, London, WC2, Great Britain
LL	Gosudarstvennaia Biblioteka SSSR imeni V.I. Lenina, pr. Kalinina 3, Moskva, Tsentr, USSR
LNH	British Museum (Natural History), Cromwell Rd., London SW7, Great Britain
LNHT	Howard-Tilton Memorial Library, Tulane University, New Orleans, Louisiana 70118
LO	Institut national des langues et civilsations orientales, Bibliothèque, 2, rue de Lille, 75007 — Paris France
LOS	School of Oriental & African Studies, University of London, Malet St., London WC1, Great Britain
LSC	Science Museum Library, South Kensington, London SW7, Great Britain
LSL	School of Slavonic & East European Studies, University of London, Senate House, London WC1, Great Britain
LU	Library, Louisiana State University, Baton Rouge, Louisiana 70803
LU	University Library, University of London, Senate House, London WC1, Great Britain

LUC	University College, University of London, Gower St., London WC1, Great Britain
LVA	Victoria & Albert Museum Library, Brompton Rd., London SW7, Great Britain
LvovGB	L'vovskaia gosudarstvennaia nauchnaia biblioteka Akademii nauk SSSR, ul. Stefanika, 2, L'vov, USSR
LvovGU	Nauchnaia Biblioteka L'vovskogo Gosudarstvennogo Universiteta, ul. Dragomanova, 5, L'vov, USSR
LvU	Harold Cohen Library, University of Liverpool, P.O. Box 123, Ashton Street, Liverpool, Great Britain
LWI	Warburg Institute, University of London, Imperial Institute Buildings, South Kensington, London SW7, Great Britain
Ly	Bibliothèque inter-universitaire de Lyn. Administration. 43, Boulevard du 11-Novembre, 69621 — Villeurbanne, France
MA	Robert Frost Library, Amherst College, Amherst, Massachusetts 01002
MB	Boston Public Library, 666 Boylston St., Box 286, Boston, Massachusetts 02117
MBAt	Boston Athenaeum, 10½ Beacon St., Boston, Massachusetts 02108
MChB	Library, Boston College, Chestnut Hill, Massachusetts 02167
MCM	MIT Libraries, Rm 145-216, Massachusetts Institute of Technology, Cambridge, Massachusetts 02139
MdBJ	Milton Eisenhower Library, Johns Hopkins University, Baltimore, Maryland 21218
MdBP	Enoch Pratt Free Library, 400 Cathedral St., Baltimore, Maryland 21201
MdBWA	Walters Art Gallery Library, 600 N. Charles St., Baltimore, Maryland 21201
MdU	Library, University of Maryland at College Park, College Park, Maryland 20742
MeB	Bowdoin College Library, Brunswick, Maine 04011
MeU	Raymond H. Folger Library, University of Maine at Orono, Orono, Maine 04473
MGU	Nauchnaia Biblioteka imeni A.M. Gor'kogo Moskovskogo Gosudarstvennogo Universiteta imeni M.L. Lomonosova, Proskpet Marksa, 20, Moskva, USSR
MH	Widener Library, Harvard University, Cambridge, Massachusetts 02138

MH-AH	Andover-Harvard Theological Library, Divinity School, Harvard University, 45 Francis Ave., Cambridge, Massachusetts 02138
MH-P	Tozzer Library, Peabody Museum of Archeology and Ethnology, Harvard University, Divinity Ave., Cambridge, Massachusetts 02138
MiD	Detroit Public Library, 5201 Woodward Ave., Detroit, Michigan 48202
MiDW	Library, Wayne State University, Detroit, Michigan 48202
MiEM	Michigan State University Library, Michigan State University, East Lansing, Michigan 48824
MiU	University Library, University of Michigan, Ann Arbor, Michigan 48109
MNS	Library, Smith College, Northampton, Massachusetts 01063
MnU	O. Meredith Wilson Library, University of Minnesota, Minneapolis, Minnesota 55455
MoSU	Pius XII Memorial Library, St. Louis University, 3655 W. Pine Blvd., St. Louis, Missouri 63108
MoSW	Library, Washington University, Skinner & Lindell Blvds., St. Louis, Missouri 63130
MoU	Elmer Ellis Library, University of Missouri–Columbia, Columbia, Missouri 65201
MP	Manchester Public Libraries, Reference Library, St. Peter's Square, Manchester 2, Great Britain
Mp	Bibliothèque inter-universitaire de Montpellier. Section centrale. 2, rue de l'École-Mage. 34008 — Montpellier CEDEX, France
MtBC	Roland R. Renne Library, Montana State University at Bozeman, Bozeman, Montana 59717
MtU	Maureen & Mike Mnasfield Library, University of Montana at Missoula, Missoula, Montana 59812
MU	Library, University of Massachusetts at Amherst, Amherst, Massachusetts 01002
MU	Muséum National d'Historie Naturelle. Bibliothèque centrale. 36, rue Geoffroy-Saint-Hilaire, 75005 — Paris, France
MWelC	Margaret Clapp Library, Wellesley College, Wellesley, Massachusetts 02181
MWiW	Sawyer Library, Williams College, Williamstown, Massachusetts 01267
N	New York State Library, Cultural Education Center, Albany, New York 12230

N	Bibliothèque inter-universitaire de Nancy. Section centrale. 11, place Carnot, 54042 — Nancy CEDEX, France
NB	Brooklyn Public Library, Grand Army Plaza, Brooklyn, New York, 11238
NBC	Library, Brooklyn College, Bedford Ave., & Ave. H., Brooklyn New York 11210
NbU	Don L. Love Memorial Library, University of Nebraska–Lincoln, Lincoln, Nebraska 68588
NBuU	Lockwood Memorial Library, SUNY Buffalo, 3435 Main St., Buffalo, New York 14214
NcD	William R. Perkins Library, Duke University, Durham, North Carolina 27706
NcGU	Walter Clinton Jackson Library, University of North Carolina at Greensboro, Greensboro, North Carolina 27412
NcRS	D.H. Hill Library, North Carolina State University, P.O. Box 5002, Raleigh, North Carolina 27607
NcU	Louis Round Wilson Library, University of North Carolina at Chapel Hill, Chapel Hill, North Carolina 27514
NFQC	Library, Queens College, 65-30 Kissena Blvd., Flushing, New York 11367
Nh	New Hampshire State Library, 20 Park St., Concord, New Hampshire 03301
NHC	Everett Needham Case Library, Colgate University, Hamilton, New York 13346
NhD	Library, Dartmouth College, Hanover, New Hampshire 03755
NHu	Huntington Public Library, 338 Main St., Huntington, New York 11743
NIC	Olin Library, Cornell University, Ithaca, New York 14850
NjP	Princeton University Libraries, Princeton University, P.O. Box 190, Princeton, New Jersey 08540
NjPT	Speer Library, Princeton Theological Seminary, Mercer St. & Library Pl., P.O. Box 111, Princeton, New Jersey 08540
NjR	Library, Rutgers University, College Ave., New Brunswick, New Jersey 08901
NmU	Library, University of New Mexico, Albuquerque, New Mexico 87131
NN	New York Public Library, Fifth Ave. & 42nd St., New York, New York 10013
NNC	Columbia University Libraries, Columbia University, New York, New York 10027

NNM	Library, American Museum of Natural History, 79th St. & Central Park, New York, New York 10024
NNMM	Thomas J. Watson Memorial Library, Metropolitan Museum of Art, Fifth Ave. & 82nd St., New York, New York 10028
NNU	Elmer Holmes Bobst Library, New York University, 70 Washington Sq. South, New York, New York 10012
NNUT	Library, Union Theological Seminary, 3041 Broadway, New York, New York 10027
NPurMC	Library, Manhattanville College, Purchase, New York 10577
NPV	Library, Vassar College, Raymond Ave., Poughkeepsie, New York 12601
NRU	Rush Rhees Library, University of Rochester, Rochester, New York 14627
NSyU	Ernest S. Bird Library, Syracuse University, 222 Waverly Ave., Syracuse, New York 13210
O	Bodleian Library, University of Oxford, Oxford, OX1 3B6 Great Britain
OA	Asmolean Museum of Art & Archaeology, University of Oxford, Beaumont St., Oxford, Great Britain
OAkU	Bierce Library, University of Akron, Akron, Ohio 44325
OCl	Cleveland Public Library, 325 Superior Ave., Cleveland, Ohio 44114
OClMA	Cleveland Museum of Art, 11150 East Blvd., Cleveland, Ohio 44106
OClW	Case Western Reserve University Library, 11161 E Blvd., Cleveland, Ohio 44106
OClW-H	Cleveland Health Sciences Library, Case Western Reserve University, Cleveland, Ohio 44106
OCU	Library, University of Cincinnati, University & Woodside, Cincinnati, Ohio 45221
OdessaGB	Odesskaia Gosudarstvennaia Nauchnaia Biblioteka imeni M. Gor'kogo, ul. Pastera, 13, Odessa, USR
OdessaGU	Nauchnaia Biblioteka Odesskogo Gosudarstvennogo Universiteta imeni I.I. Mechnikova, ul. Sovetskoi Armii, 24, Odessa, USSR
OKentU	Library, Kent State University, Kent, Ohio 44242
OkS	Library, Oklahoma State University, Stillwater, Oklahoma 74074
OkU	William Bennett Bizzell Memorial Library, University of Oklahoma, 401 W. Brooks, Norman, Oklahoma 73019

OO	Library, Oberlin College, Oberlin, Ohio 44074
OOxM	Edgar W. King Library, Miami University, Oxford, Ohio 45056
OrCS	William Jasper Kerr Library, Oregon State University, Corvaillis, Oregon 97331
OrP	Library Association of Portland, 801 SW Tenth Ave., Portland, Oregon 97205
OrPR	E.V. Hauser Memorial Library, Reed College, Portland, Oregon 97225
OrPS	Bradford Price Millar Library, Portland State University, 934 SW Harrison, P.O. Box 1151, Portland, Oregon 97207
OrU	Library, University of Oregon, Eugene, Oregon 97403
OT	Taylor Institution, University of Oxford, Oxford, OX1 3NA Great Britain
OU	William Oxley Thompson Memorial Library, Ohio State University, 1858 Neil Ave. Mall, Columbia, Ohio 43210
P	Bibliothèque de l'Université de Poitiers. 92, Avenue du Recteur-Pineau, 86034 — Poitiers CEDEX, France
PBm	Canady Library, Bryn Mawr College, Bryn Mawr, Pennsylvania 19010
PCamA	Alliance College Library, Washington Hall, Fullerton Ave., Cambridge Springs, Pennsylvania 16403
PP	Free Library of Philadelphia, Logan Square, Philadelphia, Pennsylvania 19103
PPAmP	Library, American Philosophical Society, 105 S. 5th St., Philadelphia, Pennsylvania 19106
PPAN	Library, Academy of Natural Sciences of Philadelphia, 19th & The Parkway, Philadelphia, Pennsylvania 19103
PPDrop	Library, Dropsie University, Broad & York Sts., Philadelphia, Pennsylvania 19132
PPiD	Duquesne University Library, 600 Forbes Ave., Pittsburgh, Pennsylvania 15219
PPiU	Hillman Library, University of Pittsburgh, Pittsburgh, Pennsylvania 15260
PPL	Library Company of Philadelphia, 1314 Locust St., Philadelphia, Pennsylvania 19107
PPLT	Krauth Memorial Library, Lutheran Theological Seminary, 7301 Germantown Ave., Philadelphia, Pennsylvania 19119

PPPM	Marian Angell Boyer Library, Philadelphia Museum of Art, 26th St. & Ben Franklin Parkway, P.O. Box 7646, Philadelphia, Pennsylvania 19101
PPT	Samuel Paley Library, Temple University, Berks & 13th St., Philadelphia, Pennsylvania 19122
PPULC	Union Library Catalogue of the Philadelphia Metropolitan Area, 3420 Walnut Street, Philadelphia, Pennsylvania 19174
PSC	McCabe Library, Swarthmore College, Swarthmore, Pennsylvania 19081
PSt	Fred Lewis Pattee Library, Pennsylvania State University, University Park, Pennsylvania 16802
PU	University of Pennsylvania Libraries, 3420 Walnut Street, Philadelphia, Pennsylvania 19174
PU-F	H.H. Furness Memorial Library, University of Pennsylvania, Philadelphia, Pennsylvania 19104
PU-MU	University Museum, University of Pennsylvania, 33rd & Spruce Sts., Philadelphia, Pennsylvania 19174
RPB	John D. Rockefeller Jr. Library, Brown University, Providence, Rhode Island 02912
S	Bibliothèque Nationale et Universitaire. 6, Place de la République, 67070 — Strasbourg CEDEX, France
SaU	University Library, St. Andrews University, St. Andrews, Fife, Scotland, Great Britain
ScU	Thomas Cooper Library, University of South Carolina, 1600 Sumter St., Columbia, South Carolina 29208
Slils	Institut de languages et littératures slaves. Palais Universitaire, 67000 — Strasbourg, France
SS	Gosudarstvennaia Publichnaia Biblioteka imeni Saltykova-Shchedrina, Sadovaia 18, Leningrad, USSR
SU	University Library, Sheffield University, Western Bank, Sheffield 10, Great Britain
TNJ	Joint University Libraries, 419 21st Ave. S, Nashville, Tennessee 37203
TNJ-R	Joint University Libraries, Vanderbilt School of Religion, Nashville, Tennessee 37203
TU	James D. Hoskins Library, University of Tennessee, Knoxville, Tennessee 37916
TxDaM-P	Perkins School of Theology, Southern Methodist University, Dallas, Texas 75222
TxHR	Fondren Library, William Marsh Rice University, 6100 Main St., Houston, Texas 77005
TxLT	Library, Texas Tech University, Lubbock, Texas 79409

TxU	Mirabeau B. Lasmar Library, University of Texas, Box P, Austin, Texas 78712
UAA	Bibliothèque d'Art et Archéologie, 3, rue Michelet, 75006 — Paris, France
UDC	Bibliothèque de Documentation Internationale Contemporaine, 2, rue de Rouen, 92000 — Nanterre, France
UPB	Harold B. Lee Library, Brigham Young University, University Hill, Provo, Utah 84602
US	Bibliothèque de la Sorbonne. 47, rue des Écoles, 75230 — Paris DECEX 05, France
USLsl	Institut d'Études Slaves. Bibliothèque. 9, rue Michelet, 75006 — Paris, France
UU	Marriott Library, University of Utah, Salt Lake City, Utah 84112
ViBlbV	Carol M. Newman Library, Virginia Polytechnic Institute, Blacksburg, Virginia 24061
ViFbE	United States Army Engineer School, Fort Belvoir, Virginia 22060
VilGU	Nauchnaia Biblioteka Vil'niusskogo Gosudarstvennogo Universiteta imeni V. Kapsukasa, ul. Universiteta, 3, Vil'nius, USSR
ViU	Alderman Library, University of Virginia, Charlottesville, Virginia 22901
VtMiM	Egbert Starr Libraries, Middlebury College, Middlebury, Vermont 05753
VtU	Guy W. Bailey Memorial Library, University of Vermont & State Agricultural College, Burlington, Vermont 05401
WaS	Seattle Public Library, 1000 Fourth Ave., Seattle, Washington 98104
WaU	Library, University of Washington, FM-25, Seattle, Washington 98195
WU	Memorial Library, University of Wisconsin–Madison, 728 State St., Madison, Wisconsin 53706
WvU	University Library, West Virginia University, Morgantown, West Virginia 26506

PERIODICALS/SERIALS CITED

Academy and Literature. London. 1, 1869– (AP4.A15) DLC AU CaBVaU
IaU ICN IU MdBJ MoSW NB NcD NhD NjP NN OAkU OCl OClW
OrP PPULC PU TxU WaS *Great Britain*: AU BM BP BrP BU EU
GU LdP SaU *France*: I Mp

Acta archaeologica Carpathica. Kraków. 1, 1958– (DB350.A22) DLC CtY
IU MB NcD NN WaU

Acta Baltico-Slavica. Białystok. 1, 1964– (DK511.B25A612) DLC CaOTU
CoU CtY CU ICU InNd IU MB MY NN NNM PPiU PSt WaU

Acta Jutlandica. Aarhus. 1, 1929– AzU CaBVaU CLU CtY CU ICJ ICRL
IU LU MH MnU NN NNC OU PPULC *Great Britain*: BM BU C
LdU O *France*: I P

Akademie der Wissenschaften, Berlin. Sitzungsberichte. Berlin. 1, 1836–
(AS182.B35) DLC AzU CtY ICJ IU KU KyU MH MiU NcD NcU
NIC OClW OU RPB TxU *Great Britain*: BM *France*: BN

Akademiia nauk SSSR. Izvestiia VI seriia. Moscow. 1907– (AS262.A624
ser.6) DLC CaOTU DSI GU NNC OU *USSR*: LL

Akademiia nauk SSSR. Institut arkheologii. Arkheologicheskie otkrytiia.
Moscow. 1965– DLC CSt ICU IU MdU MH MiU MnU NcU NNC
NRU NSyU PSt ScU WU

Akademiia nauk SSSR. Institut arkheologii. Kratkie soobshcheniia o dokla-
dakh i polevykh issledovaniiakh. Moscow. 1, 1939– (DK30.A173)
DLC CaOTU CLSU CLU CtY CU IaU ICU IU KU MoU NN NNC
OrU OU PPULC PSt PU RPB *USSR*: BAN GPIB LL

Akademiia nauk SSSR. Institut etnografii. Leningradskoe otdelenie. Tezisy
dokladov godichnoi nauchnoi sessii. Leningrad. v. (G58.A45) DLC
CtY *USSR*: GPIB LL

Akademiia nauk SSSR. Institut russkoi literatury. Otdel drevne-russkoi
literatury. Trudy. Moscow. 1, 1934– (PG2950.A5) DLC CaOTU
CLSU CLU CoU CtY FM InU IU KyU MH MnU NN NNC OOxM
RPB TxU WaU *Great Britain*: BM *USSR*: LL

Akademiia nauk SSSR. Institut slavianovedeniia. Kratkie soobshcheniia.
Moscow. 1951– (DK1.A33) DLC CaOTU CaQMU CLSU CLU CSt-H
CtY CU IaU IEN InU IU KU KyU MdBJ MiU NcU NIC NN NNC
OU PSt RPB TxU ViU WaU *USSR*: LL

Akademiia nauk SSSR. Otdelenie russkogo iazyka i slovesnosti. Izvestiia. Moscow. 1, 1852– (PG2013.A63) DLC CaBVaU CaOTU CtY CU DO GU IEN InU KU MH MiU NN NNC PPULC TU TxU WaU *USSR*: LL Available from Kraus Reprint.

Akademiia nauk URSR, Kiev. Instytut arkheologii. Kratkie soobshcheniia. Kiev. 1952– (DK508.3A594) DLC CaOTU CLU DDO ICU InU IU KU MdBJ MH MH-P NN NNC NNM ViU *USSR*: GPIB LL

Akademiia nauk URSR, Kiev. Istorychna sektsiia. Zapysky. Kiev. v. (DK508.A2A362) DLC CaOTU CU ICU MH MH-P MiU NN OCl WaU *USSR*: LL

Alma Ata. Universitet. Sbornik studencheskikh nauchnykh rabot. Alma Ata. 1951– *USSR*: LL

Altertum. Berlin. 1, 1955– (DE1.A35) DLC AzU CaOTU CU CU-SB DDO IaU InNd KMK MdU MH MiU NcU NIC NjP NjR NN NNC OCU OrU PSt *Great Britain*: BM BU C LWI OA

Anthropos. Salzburg. 1, 1906– (GN1.A7) DLC AzU CaBVaU CU GU ICN KyU MH MiU NcD NcU NIC NjP OCl OrU OU *Great Britain*: BM LOS LUC *France*: BN IC MU

Anzeiger fuer slavische Philologie. Wiesbaden. 1, 1966– CaBVaU CU DDO InU IU MH MnU MoSW NcU NIC NjP NN NNC NRU WaU WU

Archeologia Polona. Warsaw. 1, 1958– (DK409.A85) DLC CtY CU ICU IU MH-P MiU OU

Archeologia Polski. Warsaw. 1, 1957– (DK409.A85) DLC CtY IU MB MoU NIC *Great Britain*: O

Archeologické rozhledy. Prague. 1, 1949– (DB200.A7) DLC CaBVaU CU DDO ICU IU NN NNC NNM WaU *Great Britain*: BlU EMA O OA Available from Kraus Reprint.

Archiv fuer Anthropologie; Voelkerforschung und kolonialen Kulturwandel. Branschweig. 1, 1866– (GN2.D32) DLC CU IaAS ICJ MiU NcD NIC NjP OClW OU PPAN PU *Great Britain*: BM BU C LAI

Archiv fuer Landeskunde in den Grossherzogthuemern Mecklenburg. Schwerin. 1, 1850– MH

Archiv fuer Religionswissenschaft. Leipzig. 1, 1898– (BL4.A8) DLC CtY CU GU IaU ICU IU MH-AH MiU NIC OU WU *Great Britain*: AU C *France*: BN US

Archiv fuer slavische Philologie. Berlin. 1, 1875– (PG1.A8) DLC CtY CU ICN ICU IU MB MnU NIC NjP NN NNC OClW WU *Great Britain*: BM C GU LvU O OT *France*: BN I IC LO N S Slils US USLsl Available from Kraus Reprint.

Archiv fuer wissenschaftliche Kunde von Russland. Berlin. 1841– (DK1.A67) DLC CU CU-SC IaAS IEdS IU KyU MiU NcU NjP NN NSyU OrU OU PPiU PPULC TxU UU *Great Britain*: BM O SaU *France*: BN I MU S Also reprint by Slavistic printings and reprintings, no. 144.

Arkhiv istoriko-iuridicheskikh svedenii, otnosiashchikhsia do Rossii. Moscow. 1, 1850– DLC CaBVaU NcU NN OrU WaU WU *Great Britain*: BM *USSR*: GPIB LL

Arkiv za povjestnicu jugoslavensku. Zagreb. 1, 1851– (DB361.A6) DLC CtY MH NcU NSyU OU PU *Great Britain*: BM *France*: LO S

Athenaeum. Pismo poświęcone historyi, literaturze, szutkom. Wilno. 1, 1841– (AP 54.A83) DLC *Great Britain*: BM

Aus dem Posener Lande. Lissa. 1, 1906– MH

Ausgrabungen und Funde. Berlin. 1, 1956– (CC5.A8) DLC CU ICU MH-P MoU NN NNMM *Great Britain*: BlU BM OA

Baltische Studien. Stettin. 1, 18– (DD491.P7G4) DLC CaBVaU CLU ICJ ICN IEN IU MdBJ MH MiU NcD NIC PPULC PU *Great Britain*: O *France*: S

Bautzen, Germany. Institut za serbski ludospyt. Lětopis instituta za serbski ludospyt. Rjad C: Ludoweda. Budyšin. 1, 1953– (DD491.L3B32) DLC CLU CtY ICU IU MH NN PSt PU WaU

Bautzener Geschichtshefte. Budyšin. v. *Great Britain*: LSC

Belgrad. Etnografski muzej. Glasnik. Belgrad. 1, 1926– (DR314.A1B44) DLC CaOTU CLU MiU NcRS NcU PPiU TxU *Great Britain*: BM LFL LVA

Belgrad. Univerzitet. Filoloski fakultet. Anali. Belgrad. 1, 1961– (P19.B42) DLC InU IU KU MH NIC

Besieda. Zhurnal uchenyi, literaturny i politicheskii. Moscow. 1871– (AP50.B42) DLC CU NN *USSR*: LL Available from Inter Documentation Company.

Biblioteka warszawska. Warsaw. 1, 1841– (AP54.B5) DLC ICJ IU NN *Great Britain*: OT *USSR*: LL

Blick nach Osten. Klagenfurt. 1, 1948– (DR1.B55) DLC CaBVaU CCC CtY ICN IU MH N NNC OU PPULC PU TxU *Great Britain*: LE O

Bogoslovskii viestnik. Sergiev Posad. v. (BX460.B63) DLC ICU InU NIC NN NNC *USSR*: LL

Brussels. Université libre. Institut de philologie et d'histoire orientales et slaves. Annuaire. Brussels. 1, 1932– (PJ4.B7) DLC CtY CU IU MH MiU NNC WaU WU *Great Britain*: BlU BM BU LdU LOS LWI O

Bulgarian historical review. Sofia. 1973– (DR51.B845) DLC CLU CtY CU DDO InU IU MH MiU NIC NjP NNC RPB UU ViU WaU *Great Britain*: BM O

Bulgarska akademiia na naukite, Sofia. Arkheologicheski institut. Izvestiia. Sofia. 1, 1921– (DR51.B872) DLC COTU CLU CtY CU DDO ICU InU KyU MdBJ MH MiU NN WaU

Bŭlgarska sbirka. Sofia. 1, 1894– (AP58.B8B82) DLC CLU CtY InU IU NN PPAmP *Great Britain*: LSL

Bŭlgarsko knizhovno druzhestvo. Periodichesko spisanie. Braila. 1, 1870– (AS345.B9A2) DLC CoU CU ICU MH NBuU NN *Great Britain*: BM

Carinthia I. Mitteilungen des Geschichtsverein fuer Kaernten. Klagenfurt. 1, 1891– (DB281.C27) DLC CaBVaU CLU CtY CU MH MnU MoU NN

Česká společnost nauk, Prague. Abhandlungen. 1, 1775– (AS142.C31) DLC CtY DSI ICJ ICRL MA MdBJ NcU NIC NNC NNM NNU OCU PPAmP PPAN PU RPB WU *Great Britain*: BM

Československá akademie věd. Vestník. Prague. 1, 1891– (AS142.C41) DLC CaBVaU CLU CtY CU ICJ KU MdBJ MiU MoSW NBuU NcU NjP NNC NSyU OrCS PU Available from Kraus Reprint.

Československá etnografie. Prague. 1, 1953– (GN1.C53) DLC CLU ICRL ICU KU MH WaU *Great Britain*: BM LAI LFL O

Český lid. Prague. 1, 1892– (DB191.C45) DLC CaBVaU CtY CU ICU KU MH NcU NN NSyU OU WaU *Great Britain*: O

Dawna kutura. Breslau. 1, 1954– (DK409.D3) DLC InU IU MB NN *Great Britain*: BM

Deutsche Gesellschaft fuer Anthropologie, Ethnologie und Urgeschichte. Korrespondenz-Blatt. Braunschweig. 1, 1870– (GN2.D3) DLC CSt DSI IaU ICJ IEN MiU MnU MoU NN OClW OU TNJ TxU *France*: BN MU

Deutsche Literaturzeitung fuer Kritik der internationalen Wissenschaft. Berlin. 1, 1880– (Z1007.D48) DLC FU GU ICJ IU KyU MB MH MiU MNS MoSW NIC NjP OCl OClW OCU OrCS OrU OU PU *Great Britain*: BM C *France*: L Ly S US

Deutsches Jahrbuch fuer Volkskunde. Berlin. 1, 1955– (GR165.D4) DLC CU InU IU KU KyU MH MoU NIC OCl PU TxU *Great Britain*: C LFL LWI O

Duchovní pastýr. Měsíčnik katolického duchovenstva. Prague. v. (BX806.C9D8) DLC

Dwutygodnik naukowy. Kraków. 1878–79.

Eastern Review. Klagenfurt. 1, 1948– (DR1.E37) DLC DDO DS IU NcU NN OClW *Great Britain*: BU

Ethnologia slavica. Bratislava. 1, 1969– (GN549.S6E8) DLC CaOONM CtY CU ICU IU MH MiEM NIC NjP NNC OrU PSt PU RPB ViU WaU

Etnološki pregled. Beograd. 1, 1959– (GN1.E886) DLC CLU CU IU NIC WaU

Euhemer; przegląd religioznawczy. Warsaw. 1, 1957– (BL9.P6E8) DLC ICU IU MH NN *Great Britain*: BM

Eurasia septentrionalis antiqua. Helsingfors. 1, 1926– (GN700.E8) DLC CtY DDO ICU KU NIC NN OCl OU PU *Great Britain*: BU C LAI LCA LOS O OA *France*: LO UAA

Filologicheskiia zapiski. Voronezh. 1, 1860– DLC CtY ICU IU MH MiU NN NNC *USSR*: LL Available from Inter Documentation Company.

Finskii vestnik. See Sievernoe obozrienie.

Fontes archaeologici Posnaniense; annales musei archeologici Posnaniensis. Poznań. 1, 1950– (DK409.F6) DLC CtY CU ICU IU MB MH-P MiU NIC NN NNC NNM PU-MU *Great Britain*: BM CH EMA LAI O OA

Forschungsfragen unserer Zeit. Ergaenzungsheft. (Gisela Lienau) Zeven. NIC

Freimuethiges Abenblatt. Schwerin. 1, 1818– ICRL MH MiU

Galitsko-russkaia matitsa, Lvov. Nauchno-literaturnyi sbornik galitsko-russkoi matitsy. Lvov. 1865– NNC *USSR*: LL

Geograficheskoe obshchestvo SSSR. Zapiski po otdeleniiu etnografii. St. Petersburg. 1, 1867– (GN2.G4772) DLC CaOTU CLU CSt-H CtY CU DSI InU IU KU MH NN OrU *USSR*: LL

Germania. Frankfurt am Main. 1, 1917– (DD53.A33) DLC CtY CU ICU IU MiU NN OCU TxU *Great Britain*: BM OA *France*: BN N S US

Germanien; monatshefte fuer Germanenkunde. Berlin. 1, 1929– (DD1.G385) DLC CU ICU IU MiU NN *France*: BN

Gesellschaft fuer schleswig-holsteinische Geschichte, Kiel. Zeitschrfit. Neumuenster. 1, 1870– (DD491.S6G6) DLC CtY IaU ICU KyU MH MnU MoU NBuU NN NNC OCl PU

Globus; illustrierte Zeitschrfit fuer Laender- und Voelkerkunde. Hildburghaussen. 1861/62– (G1.G57) DLC AzU LU MB MH MiU NN OCl OU *Great Britain*: BM *France*: Mp MU S

Griefswaldisches Academisches Archiv; eine Zeitschrift. Griefswald. 1, 1816– NIC OCl *Great Britain*: BM

Gryf; pismo poświęcone sprawom kaszubsko-pomorskim. Gdańsk. 1, 1908– (DD491.P791G78) DLC IU

Harvard. University. Seminar on Ukrainian Studies. Minutes. Cambridge. 1, 1970/71– (DK508.A2H35) DLC CaOTU CSt CtU CU CU-SB ICU InU IU MH MiEM NjP NN OCl PU

Heimatbund und Geschichtsverein Herzogtum Lauenburg. Schriftreihe. Ratzeburg. 1957– MH

Historijski zbornik. Zagreb. 1, 1948– (DR301.H5) DLC CaBVaU CtY CU ICU MiU NcU NIC NjP NN NNC OU ViU Available from Kraus Reprint.

History of Religions. Chicago. 1, 1961– (BL1.H5) DLC AzU CaOTU CLU CoU CSt CU GU IaU IEN LU MdBJ MH MiU MnU NcD NIC OClW OrU OU TxU ViU *Great Britain*: BM LK MU O

Iaroslavskie eparkhial'nye vedomosti. Iaroslavl'. 1860– *USSR*: LL

Iazyk i literatura. Leningrad. 1, 1926– DLC KU NN NNC *Great Britain*: BM *USSR*: LL

Internationale Revue. Monatsschrift fuer das gesammte geistige Leben und Streben. Vienna. 1866– CtY ICN MdBJ NN *Great Britain*: BM *USSR*: LL

Istoricheskii zhurnal. Moscow. 1931– (D1.I75) DLC CaOTU CLU CSt-H CU ICU MH MiU MnU NcU NIC NN NNC OrU OU PU ScU WaU WU *USSR*: GPIB LL

Istoriia SSSR. Moscow. 1957– (DK1.A3275) DLC AzU CLSU CLU CoU
CSt-H CtY DS ICU InU IU KU LU MH MiU MoSW NcU NN NNC
NSyU OU PSt PU RPB TxHR TxU ViU WaU WU *Great Britain*: BM
LSL O *USSR*: GPIB LL

Jahrbuecher fuer Geschichte Osteuropas. Breslau. 1, 1936– (D1.J3) DLC
CaBVaU CaOTU CoU CSt CtY CU DDO GU IEN LU MH MiU
NcD NcU NIC OCU OrU *Great Britain*: BM *France*: USLsl

Jahrbuecher fuer slawische Literatur, Kunst und Wissenschaft. Leipzig. 1,
1843– (DR1.J2) DLC ICU IU NN *Great Britain*: BM

Jomsburg; Voelker und Staaten im Osten und Norden Europas. Leipzig. 1,
1937– (D1.J53) DLC CtY ICU MH MiU MnU NcD NjP NNC *Great
Britain*: BM

Journal of Byelorussian studies. London. 1, 1965– (DK507.A2J68) DLC
CaOTY CaOWA CtY CU ICU MH MiEM NIC NN *Great Britain*:
BM

Journal of Indo-European studies. Hattiesburg. 1, 1973– (CB201.J8) DLC
AzU CaBVaU CaOTU CLSU CLU CoU CSt CtY GU IaU IU KU
MH MiDW MiEM MiU MnU MoU MU NIC NNC PU ScU TxU UU
ViU VtU WaU WU *Great Britain*: O SU

Jugoslovenska akademija znanosti i umjetnosti, Zagreb. Rad. Zagreb. 1,
1867– (AS142.J7) DLC CaBVaU CU GU ICRL MH MiU NBuU NcU
NN NC OU TxU

Južnoslovenski Filolog. Beograd. 1, 1913– (PG1.J8) DLC CaBVaU CaOTU
CU OU PPiD TxU WaU *Great Britain*: BM

Kazan. Universitet. Obshchestvo arkheologii, istorii i etnografii. Izvestiia.
Kazan. 1, 1878– (AS262.K22) DLC CtY ICU MH NcD *USSR*: LL

Kharkov. Universytet. Istoriko-filologicheskoe obshchestvo. Sbornik. Kharkov. 1, 1886– (DK3.K47) DLC MH NN *USSR*: LL Available from
Inter Documentation Company.

Khristianskiia drevnosti i arkheologiia.   St. Petersburg. 1, 1862/63–
(NA4800.K47) DLC CtY DDO ICU IU NN OrU PSt *Great Britain*:
BM *USSR*: LL

Knjiga o Balkanu. Belgrad. 1, 1936– NN *USSR*: LL

Krakow. Muzeum archeologiczne. Materiały archeologiczne. Kraków. 1,
1959– (GN845.P6K7) DLC CU ICU MiU NIC

Krok. Weřegný spis wšenaučný pro vzdělance naródu českoslovanského.
Prague. 1821– *Great Britain*: BM

Kwartalnik historyczny. Lvov. 1, 1887– (D1.K85) DLC CLSU CtY IU KU MH MnU NjP NN NNC NSyU *France*: BN

Lasizische monatsschrift. Goerlitz. 1793– NjP *Great Britain*: BM

Lech; Dziennik Polski, poświęcony literaturze, dziejom oyczystym, i współczesnym. Warsaw. 1823– *Great Britain*: BM

Linguistica slovaca. Breslau. 1, 1939– (P10.L56) DLC CaBVaU CtY NIC NN NNC OU TxU WU

London. University. Warburg Institute. Journal. London. 1, 1937– (AS122.L8515) DLC AzU CaBVaU CSt CU ICN ICU InU LU MB MdBP MoSW NIC NN PSt TxU WaU *Great Britain*: BM Available from Kraus Reprint.

Lud. Lublin. 1, 1895– DLC CSt ICU IU NIC OU *Great Britain*: LFL *France*: BN

Lužica; měsačnik za zabawu a powučenje. Budyšin. 1, 1882– DLC CSt IU

Lužičan; časopis za zabawu a powučenje. Budyšin. 1, 1864– ICN *Great Britain*: BM *USSR*: GPIB

Maćica serbska, Bautzen. Časopis. 1, 1848– (PG5631.M3) DLC CtY IU MH

Maerkische Forschungen. Berlin. 1, 1841– (DD491. B81F6) DLC CSt ICU IU MH NN *Great Britain*: LU *France*: S US

Magazin der saechischen Geschichte. Dresden. 1, 1784– MH MnU *Great Britain*: BM C *France*: S

Magazyn powszechny. Wiadomosći uzytecznych i ciekawych. Paris. 1, 1833. *Great Britain*: BM

Mainzer Zeitschrift. Mainz. 1, 1906– (DD901.M2M25) DLC ICU KyU MoU *Great Britain*: C *France*: AD S

Mannus; Zeitschrift fuer Vorgeschichte. Wuerzburg. 1, 1909– (GN700.M3) DLC CtY CU ICU MdBJ MnU NIC NjP NN NNC OU TxU *Great Britain*: BM *France*: S UAA Available from Kraus Reprint.

Materiały zachodnio-pomorskie. Szczesin. 1, 1955– (DD491.P74M3) DLC CtY IU MH N NNC WU *Great Britain*: CH OA

Matica slovenská, Turčiansky Sv. Martin. Letopis. Vo Viedni. 1864– (AS142.T8) DLC CaBVaU ICU MH MiU NN NNC *Great Britain*: BM

Matice moravska, Bruenn. Sbornik. Bruenn. 1, 1869– (DB541.M3) DLC CaBVaU CoU CSt CtY ICU InU MiU NcD NjP WaU Available from Kraus Reprint.

Mecklenburgische Jahrbuecher. Schwerin. 1, 1836– DLC CtY ICU MH NIC NjP NNC NSyU

Mecklenburgische Monatshefte. Rostock. 1, 1924– NN OCl

Monatsschrift von und fuer Mecklenburg. See Neue Monatsschrift von und fuer Mecklenburg.

Moscow. Gosudarstvennyi istoricheskii muzei. Trudy. Moscow. 1, 1926– (DK1.M6) DLC CaOTU CLSU CLU CSt-H CtY DDO ICU IEN InNd InU IU KU MH MiU MoU NBC NcD NIC NjP NN NNC NNMM NRU OU RPB WaU WU *USSR*: GPIB LL

Moscow. Universitet. Obshchestvo istorii i drevnostei rossiskikh. Chteniia. Moscow. 1, 1846– (DK1.M672) DLC CaBVaU CtY CU DDO GEU NBuU OrPS OrU *USSR*: GPIB LL Available from Inter Documentation Company.

Moscow. Universitet. Obshchestvo istorii i drevnostei rossiskikh. Vremennik. Moscow. 1, 1849– (DK1.M6722) DLC CtY CU MH MiU NN NNC OrU WU *USSR*: GPIB LL

Moskovskii telegraf. Zhurnal literatury, kritiki, nauk i khozhestv. Moscow. 1825– (AP65.M64) DLC CtY IU NcD NN NNC *Great Britain*: BM *USSR*: LL

Moskovskiia uchenyia viedomosti. Moscow. 1805– *USSR*: LL

Moskovskiia viedomosti. Moscow. 1756– DLC MH N *Great Britain*: BM *USSR*: LL

Moskovskoe arkheologicheskoe obshchestvo. Drevnosti; trudy Moskovskogo arkheologicheskogo obshchestva. Moscow. 1865– (DK1.M5824) DLC CSt CtY CU ICU IU NN NNC PPAmP *Great Britain*: BM *USSR*: GPIB LL

Moskovskoe arkheologicheskoe obshchestvo. Zapiski. Moscow. 18– DLC *Great Britain*: BM *USSR*: GPIB LL

Movoznavstvo; naukovi zapysky. Kiev. 1, 1941– (PG3801.A415) DLC CaAEU CaOTU CLU CtY CU ICU InU IU MH MiU NcD NcU NIC NjR NN NNC NSyU PPiU WaU WU *Great Britain*: BM C *USSR*: LL

Mówią wieki; magazyn historyczny. Warsaw. v. (DK401.P889) DLC MH N *Great Britain*: BM

Muzejsko društvo za Slovenijo, Ljubljana. Glasnik. Ljubljana. Glasnik. Ljubljana. 1, 1919/20– (DR381.S6M8) DLC CaBVaU CSt CU IU MoU NIC NN NNC *Great Britain*: BM LNH

Naples. Instituto orientale. Sezione slava. Annali. Naples. 1, 1958–
(PG1.N35) DLC CaOTU CaOTY CLU CSt CtY CU ICU IU KU
MH MiU MoSW NIC NjP NN OU PU WU

Narodno stvaralaštvo. Folklor. Belgrad. 1, 1962– CaOOU CLU CU

Narodopisný sborník českoslovanský. Prague. 1, 1897– (GN1.N3) DLC CtY
CU ICU InU MB MiU NcU *Great Britain*: BM LFL *France*: USLsl
Available from Kraus Reprint.

Nastavni vjesnik. Zagreb. 1, 1892– (L51.N37) DLC CtY IU KU MH MnU
NIC NNC ViU WaU *USSR*: LL

Nederlands Filologen-Congres. Handelingen. Groningen. v. (P21.N43) DLC
MH NIC NN NNC OU PU TxU

Neue Monatsschrift von und fuer Mecklenburg. Schwerin. 1, 1788– MH
NN 1788–91 as Monatsschrift von fuer Mecklenburg.

Neues Archiv fuer saechische Geschichte und Altertumskunde. Dresden. 1,
1880– (DD801.S31A7) DLC CtY CU DSI ICU MdBJ MH MnU NN
NNC OCl PPAmP RPB *Great Britain*: BM

Neues Lausitzisches Magazin. Goerlitz. 1822–

Nezhin, Ukraine. Istoriko-filologicheskii institut kniazia Bezborodko. Izvestiia. Nezhin. 1, 1877– CtY NN *USSR*: LL

Niwa dwutygodnik; poświęcony sprawom społecznym, naukowym i lite-
rackim. Warsaw. 1, 18– NN

Nizhegorodskiia eparkhial'nye viedomosti. Nizhnii-Novgorod. 1864–

Notatki Płockie; pismo regionale Mazowsza płockiego. Płock. 1, 1956–
(DK651.P59N57) DLC MH

Novgorodskii gosudarstvenny istoricheskii muzei. Materialy i issledovaniia.
Novgorod. 1, 1930– *USSR*: LL

Novi dni. Toronto. 1, 1950– (AP58.U5N5) DLC CaSSU CSt-H IU NN

Obzor praehistorický. Praha. 1, 1922– (GN808.C903) DLC CtY ICF ICU
IU MH-P MiU NIC NN PU

Odesskoe obshchestvo istorii i drevnostei. Zapiski. Odessa. 1, 1844– DLC
CtY ICU InU IU MiU NN PU *Great Britain*: BM *USSR*: LL

Offa; Berichte und Mitteilungen. Neumuenster in Holstein. 1, 1936–
(DD51.3035) DLC CtY CU NN *Great Britain*: OA

Onomastica. Wrocław. 1, 1955– (G104.057) DLC CtY CU ICU IU MB
MH MiU NcD NcU NN TxHR *Great Britain*: LSL

Orol; Časopis pre zábavu a poučenie. Turčiansky Sv. Martin. 1, 1870– IU
MH NN *USSR*: LL

Ostmecklenburgische Heimat. Halbmonatszeitschrift fuer ostmecklenburgische Heimatwerte, Landeskunde und Unterhaltung. Teterow. 1928–39.

Otechestveniia zapiski. St. Petersburg. 1818– (AP50.085) DLC CaBVaU
CaOTU CLSU CLU CSt CtY CU ICU InU IU KU MH MiU NcU
NN NNC NSyU OU TxU *Great Britain*: BM *USSR*: LL Available
from Inter Documentation Company.

Pam'iatnyki Ukrainy. Kiev. v. (N9012.U4P3) DLC *USSR*: LL

Paris. Ecole pratique des hautes etudes. Centre d'etudes pre et protohistoriques. Antiquitates nationales et internationales. Paris. v. 1960– DLC
CaOTRM CtY DSI MH-P MoU NN *Great Britain*: BlU *France*: BN

Polska Akademia Nauk. Oddział w Krakowie. Sprawozdania. Kraków. 1,
1957–DLC CaOTU CLU CtY CU IU MH MiU N NN NNC RPB WU

Polska Akademia Umiejetnosci, Kraków. Bulletin international. Kraków.
1889– (AS142.K83) DLC IaAS ICJ ICU MiU MnU NIC NjP NN NNC
OU RPB WaU *Great Britain*: BM GU LNH O

Polska Akademia Umiejętności, Kraków. Sprawozdania z czynności i
posiedzen. Kraków. 1, 1896– (AS142.K82) DLC CaBVaU ICJ InU
KU MnU NN NNC OCl PU *Great Britain*: BM *France* : BN I

Polska Akademia Umiejętności, Krakow. Komisja antropologiczna. Materyały antropologiczno-archeologiczne i etnograficzne. Kraków. 1,
1896– (GN2.P582) DLC CU ICJ ICU PU-MU WaU

Pommersche Jahrbuecher. Griefswald. 1, 1900– CtY CU ICU MH MnU NjP
Great Britain: BM LVA

Prace filologiczne. Warsaw. 1, 1885– (P9.P7) DLC CSt ICU IU KU MH N
NRU TxU ViU *Great Britain*: BU LSL *France*: BN Available from
Inter Documentation Company.

Praehistorische Zeitschrift. Berlin. 1, 1909–(GN700.P825) DLC CaBVaU
CoU ICJ KU LU MH MiU NIC NjP NN OCU ViU *Great Britain*:
BM LAI *France*: BN S UAA Available from Kraus Reprint.

Prague. Národní museum. Časopis. Prague. 1, 1827–(AS142.C23) DLC
CaBVaU CSt CU GU ICRL ICU InU IU KU MB MH MiU MoU
NcU NIC NN NSyU OrCS OU PU ViU *Great Britain*: LSL Available
from Kraus Reprint.

Prague. Národní museum. Monatsschrift der Gesellschaft des vaterlaendischen Museums in Boehmen. Prague. 1, 1827– (AS142.C22) DLC CaBVaU ICU *Great Britain*: BM C LNH *France*: MU

Pravoslavnyi sobesiednik. Kazan. 1, 1855– (BX460.P76) DLC CU ICU IU KU MH N TNJ-R *USSR*: LL Available from Inter Documentation Company.

Prilozi za književnost, jezik, istoriju i folklor. Belgrad. 1, 1921– (PG560.P7) DLC CaBVaU CtY CU KU LU MiU NjP NNC OU *Great Britain*: BM LSL Available from Kraus Reprint.

Priroda a spoločnost'. Martin. v. (AS141.P7) DLC ICRL NN

Przegląd historyczny. Warsaw. 1, 1905– (DK401.P915) DLC AAP CaBVaU CLU ICRL IU KU MiU NBuU NcD NjP NSyU OU PSt TxU WaU *Great Britain*: BM O *France*: BN UDC USLsl

Przegląd tygodniowy zycia społecznego, literatury. Warsaw. 1, 1866– *Great Britain*: BM

Przegląd zachodni. Poznań. 1, 1945– (DK401.P925) DLC CaBVaU CSt-H IU MB MH NBuU NN NNC NSyU OCU TxU WU *Great Britain*: LSL O Available from Kraus Reprint.

Przegląd zachodnio-pomorski. Szczecin. 1957– (DD491.P71P74) DLC

Przyjaciel ludzi. Leszno. 1, 1834– IU NNC *Great Britain*: BM *USSR*: GPIB

Quaestiones Medii Aevi. Warszawa. 1, 1977– (D111.Q34) DLC AzU DeU InU MH NcU NIC

Revue anthropologique. Paris. 1, 1891– (GN2.P25) DLC CaOTU CU ICJ ICU IU KU LU MB MH MiU MnU NcU NjP NN NNC OClW PU ViU *Great Britain*: BM LAI *France*: BN

Revue archéologique. Paris. 1, 1844– (CC3.R4) DLC CaBVaU CaOTU CtU CtY GU ICN InU MB MdBP MiU NcD NcU NhD NjP OClW OCU OU PU *Great Britain*: BM CAN MP O *France*: BN I L Ly S UAA US

Revue d'histoire et de philosophie religieuses. Paris. 1, 1921– (BR3.R33) DLC AzU CLU CSt CU DDO GEU GU ICU IU MB MH MoSW NhD NNC NSyU OrU OU TxU ViU *Great Britain*: AU BM O *France*: BN Bx I S US Available from Kraus Reprint.

Revue de l'histoire des religions. Paris. 1, 1880– (BL3.R4) DLC AzU CLU CoU CtY CU GU ICN LU MB MH NN NSyU PU WaU *Great Britain*: BM C MP O *France*: BN LO Ly Mp S Available from Kraus Reprint.

Revue des études slaves. Paris. 1, 1921– (PG1.R4) DLC CaOTU GEU GU
ICU IU KyU MB MH MiU MoSW NBuU NcU NN OCl OU PSt PU
Great Britain: BM BU C LVA LvU SU *France*: BN I LO Ly N P S US
USLsl

Ricerche slavistiche. Rome. 1, 1952– (DR25.R5) DLC CaBVaU CtY CU
ICU NN OrU OU TU TxU *Great Britain*: BU

Rozhlad. Časopis za serbsku kulturu. Budyšin. 1, 1950– (AP58.W4R6) DLC
CaQMU CLU ICU InU IU *Great Britain*: BM O

Russia. Ministerstvo narodnogo prosveshcheniia. Zhurnal. St. Petersburg.
1, 1834– (L451.A55) DLC IU NIC *Great Britain*: BM *USSR*: GPIB
LL Available from Inter Documentation Company.

Russkaia besieda. Moscow. 1856– (AP50.R79) DLC CaOTU CSt NcU NjR
NN NNC WaU *Great Britain*: BM *USSR*: LL

Russkaia literatura; istoriko-literaturnyi zhurnal. Leningrad. 1, 1958–
(PG2900.R85) DLC CaQMU CLU ICRL IU MdBJ MH MoU PSt
RPB ViU WU *Great Britain*: BM OT *USSR*: LL

Russkii filologicheskii vestnik. Warsaw-Moscow-St. Petersburg. 1, 1879–
(PG2003.R84) DLC CtY MH *Great Britain*: MU *USSR*: LL Available
from Inter Documentation Company

Russkii fol'klor. Moscow. 1, 1956– (GR190.R86) DLC CaOTU CLU CU
ICRL ICU IU LU MnU MoU NcD NhD NIC PSt *Great Britain*: BM
USSR: LL

Russkii istoricheskii sbornik. Moscow. 1, 1837– (DK1.M6725) DLC CU
MH NN *Great Britain*: BM *USSR*: LL

Saeculum. Jahrbuch fuer universal Geschichte. Freiburg. 1, 1950– (D2.S3)
DLC CaBVaU MH N NNC OrU ViU WaU *Great Britain*: EU LB LE
O Available from Kraus Reprint.

Sarajevo. Zemaljski muzej. Glasnik. Sarajevo. 1, 1889– (AM101.S256) DLC
CaBVaU CSt CU DSI ICU InU KU MiU NNC NNM NSyU OCl ViU

Saxonia. Zeitschrift fuer geschichts- altertums- und Landeskunde des
koenigreichs Sachsen. Leipzig. 1, 1875/76– CtY *Great Britain*: BM

Scientific American supplement. New York. 1, 1876– (T1.S52) DLC CaBVa
CaBVaU CaQMM CoG CoU CSt CtU CtW CtY DSI FJ FTaSU ICJ
ICRL KyU MdBP MH MoSW MtU NBuU NcD NcRS Nh NHC NIC
NjP NjR OCU OrCS OrP OrPS PP PPL PU RPB ViFbE WaS WvU

Sem'ia i shkola; pedagogicheskii zhurnal. St. Petersburg. 1871– (L51.S4) DLC NN *USSR*: LL Available from Inter Documentation Company.

Serbska pratyja za dolnych Serbow. Budyšin. v. (AY859.W35S4) DLC NN

Serbska protyka. Bautzen. v. (AY859.W35S45) DLC

Sievernaia pchela. Gazeta politicheskaia i literaturnaia. St. Petersburg. 1825– CaOTU MH NIC *Great Britain*: BM *USSR*: LL Available from Inter Documentation Company.

Sievernoe obozrienie. St. Petersburg. 1, 1845– CtY IU *USSR*: LL 1845–47 as Finskii vestnik. Ucheno-literaturnyi zhurnal. Available from Inter Documentation Company.

Slavia; Časopis pro slovanskou filologii. Prague. 1, 1922– (PG1.S6) DLC CaBVaU CaOTU CLU CSt CU DDO ICU KU LU MiU NcD NIC NN PU ViU WaU *Great Britain*: BM C LSL *France*: I L LO US USLsl Available from Inter Documentation Company and Kraus Reprint.

Slavia antiqua. Poznań. 1, 1945– (D147.S5) DLC CaBVaU CaSSU CtY CU DDO ICU IU KU LU MH MiU MoU NIC NN NNM PU TxU ViU WU *Great Britain*: GU LAI *France*: BN

Slavia occidentalis. Poznań. 1, 1921– (D377.A1S56) DLC CoU CSt CtY IaU InU IU KU MdBP MH NIC NjP NN NNC NSyU OU PU TxU WaU WU *Great Britain*: LSL *France*: BN LO USLsl

Slavic Review. Menasha. 1945– (D377.A1A5) DLC AU AzU CLSU CSt CtY CU DeU GEU IaU ICN ICU IEN InU IU LU MB MdBJ MH MiDW MNS MnU MoSU MtU MWelC NIC NjP NjR NN NNC OCl OkU OOxM PBm PPiU PSt PU RPB TxDaM TxU UU WaU WU *Great Britain*: AbU BM BP BU C EU GU LU OT

Slavica Gandensia. Ghent. 1, 1974– CaBVaU CaOTU CLU CSt CtY IaU ICU InU IU MH MnU NIC NjP NNC TxU WaU

Slavica Hierosolymitana. Jerusalem. 1, 1977– (PG1.S623) DLC CSt CU IEN MiU MnU NIC NN PU RPB

Slovanský sborník. Prague. 1, 1881– CaBVaU CaQMU CoU CU ICU InU IU MiU NcU NIC NNC *Great Britain*: BM *France*: BN Available from Kraus Reprint.

Slovenska archeologia. Bratislava. 1, 1953– (DB670.S5) DLC CaBVaU CLU CU ICU IU MyU MH-P NIC NN NNC PU-MU ViU *Great Britain*: C CH EMA LAI OA

Slovenski etnograf. Ljubljana. 1, 1948– (GN1.S5) DLC CLU CSt CtY ICRL ICU KU MH MiU NIC NN NNC OU WaU WU *Great Britain*: BM LAI Available from Kraus Reprint.

Social Science. Moscow. 1, 1970– DLC CaAEU CaBVaU CaMWU CaNBFU CaOOCC CaOONM CaOWtU CLU CoU CSt-H CtU CtY CU CURiv FTaSU FU GASU IaU ICU IEN InU IU KU MB MCM MdU MH MiEM MiU MU NcD NIC NjP NN NNC PPiU PPT PSC TxU VtU WaU WU *USSR*: LL Exists in various languages.

Sofia. Naroden etnografski muzei. Izvestiia. Sofia. 1, 1921– (GN1.S6) DLC CU NN

Sovetskaia arkheologiia. Moscow. 1, 1936– (DK30.A17) DLC AzU CaB-VaU CLU CSt CtY ICRL ICU IU KU MiU MnU MoSW N NRU OrU OU ViU WU *Great Britain*: BM LWI *USSR*: GPIB LL Available from Inter Documentation Company.

Sovetskaia etnografiia. Moscow. 1, 1931– (GN1.S65) DLC AzU CaBVaU CaOTU CSt CI ICU IU KU MdBJ MH MiU NcD NcU NN NNC NSyU OCl OrU OU PU TxU WaU *Great Britain*: BM *USSR*: GPIB LL Available from Inter Documentation Company.

Sovetskoe slavianovedenie. Moscow. 1, 1965– (D377.A1S74) DLC CaOTU CLU ICRL ICU InU IU MH MiU MoSW NIC NNC OO RPB TxU WaU WU *Great Britain*: BU *USSR*: GPIB LL

Soviet anthropology and archeology. White Plains. N. Y. 1, 1962–(GN1.S66) DLC AzTeS AzU C CaBVaU CaBViV CaMWU CaOKQ CaOTU CaOWA CaQMM CaQMU CCC CLU CNoS CtW CtY CU CU-SB GEU IaU ICU IEdS IEN InLP InNd InU IU KyU LNHT MH-P MnU MiEM MiU MoSW NBC NcD NcRS NcU NhD NIC NjP NN NRU OClW OCU OkS OrU PPiU PSt PU RPB TxU UU ViU VtU WaU WU *Great Britain*: CH LAI LE OA SU

Srpska akademija nauk i umetnosti, Belgrad. Etnografski institut. Glasnik. 1, 1952– (GN2.S943) DLC CaBVaU CLU CSt ICU IU MiU NIC

Starohravatska prosvjeta. Knih. Zagreb. 1, 1949– (DB370.5S8) DLC CSt CU DDO MH MoU OrU OU ViU WU

Staroslovan; Vierteljahrsschrift zur Pfleg der altslavischen Sprache, Ge-schichte und Kultur. Kremsier. 1, 1913– (PG1.S7) DLC CSt ICU IU MH NIC NN NNC *Great Britain*: BM C Available from Kraus Reprint.

Studi e materiali di storia delle religioni. Rome. 1, 1925– (BL5.S8) DLC CU IaU ICU KU MB MH-AH MiU NcD NIC NN OCU PU TxU *Great Britain*: BM LFL LWI O *France*: US

Studia slavica. Budapest. 1, 1955– (PG1.S8) DLC CaBVaU IU KU MB NIC NSyU OrU ViU *Great Britain*: BM C OT

Studia ucrainica. Ottawa. 1, 1978– (DK508.S78) DLC CaAEU ICU IU MH MiU MnU NIC

Światowit. Warsaw. 1, 1899– (GN823.A1) DLC oU CtY CU ICU KU KyU MiU MoU NIC NNC NNM PSt *Great Britain*: BM LAI *France*: BN

Synthèses. Brussels. 1, 1946– (AP22.S9) DLC CaBVaU CSt CtY GU IaU ICU InU IU MB MdBJ MH MiU NN NNC OrU TxU WaU

Tartu, Ülikool. Trudy po znakovym sistemam. Tartu. 1, 1964– (AS262.T22A25) DLC CtY IU MiU NIC *USSR*: LL

Towarzystwo naukowe Krakowskie. Rocznik. Kraków. 1, 1817– (AS142.K984) DLC CtY ICRL InU IU MiU

Towarzystwo naukowe w Toruniu. Roczniki. Toruń. 1, 1878– CSt CtY ICU IU MB MiU NcD NN NND WaU

Towarzystwo naukowe w Toruniu. Wydział nauk historycznych, prawniczych i społecznych. Zapiski historyczne; kwartalnik poświęcony historii Pomorza. Toruń. 1, 1908– (DD491.P71T6) DLC CaBVaU CSt-H CtY ICN ICRL IU KU LU NcD NN NNC OU WU *USSR*: LL

Towarzystwo warszawskie przyjaciol nauk. Roczniki. Warsaw. 1, 1802– (AS262.W29) DLC *Great Britain*: BM

Trudy russkikh uchenykh za-granitsei; sbornik akademicheskoi gruppy v Berline. Berlin. 1, 1922– (AS181.T7) DLC ICJ IU MH NN NNC OU PU *Great Britain*: BM

Ukrains'kyi istorychnyi zhurnal. Kiev. 1, 1957– (DK508.A2U68) DLC CaBVaU CLU CoU CU ICU InU IU KU KyU MH MiEM MiU MnU NIC NN OCU WaU *Great Britain*: LSL O *USSR*: GPIB LL

Unser Pommerland. Monatsschrift fuer das Kulturleben der Heimat. Stargard. 1912–37.

Urainia; Monatsschrift ueber Natur und Gesellschaft. Jena. 1, 1924– NN NNM PU

Das Vaterland der Sachsen. Mitteilungen aus Sachsens Vorzeit und Gegenwart. Dresden. 1, 1838– *Great Britain*: BM *USSR*: LL

Verein fuer kaschubische Volkskunde, Karthaus. Mitteilungen. Leipzig. 1, 1908– CtY ICU MH NN OCl *Great Britain*: C O

Vestnik drevnei istorii. Moscow. 1, 1937– (D51.A423) DLC AzU CLSU CLU CSt CSt-H CtY CU DDO DS FU ICU InNd IU KU MB MdBJ MH MiU MnU MoU N NbU NBuU NcD NcU NIC NjP NN NNC

NNMM OCl PPiU PPULC PU RPB WaU *Great Britain*: BM *France*: BN *USSR*: GPIB LL

Vestnik Evropy. Moscow. 1, 1802– DLC NN *Great Britain*: BM *USSR*: LL Available from Inter Documentation Company.

Voprosy iazykoznaniia. Moscow. 1952– (P9.V6) DLC CaBVaU CtY DS ICRL IEN InU IU MdBJ MH MnU NIC PU *Great Britain*: BU LO *USSR*: LL

Voprosy istorii. Moscow. 1945– (D1.V6) DLC CaAEU CaBVaU COTU CaSSU CLU CSt-H CtY CU IaU ICN ICU IEN IU KU LU MdBJ MH MoSW NcD NIC NN NNC NRU OU PU RPB TxU WaU *Great Britain*: BM GU O *USSR*: GPIB LL Available from Inter Documentation Company.

Voprosy istorii. Mezhvuzovskii sbornik. Minsk. 1974– (DK507.A2V66) DLC CSt MiU MnU

Voprosy slavianskogo iazykoznaniia. Moscow. 1, 1954– (PG1.V6) DLC CaAEU CaBVaU CaOTU CaSSU CoU CtY CU IaU ICRL ICU InU IU KU LU MiU MnU NjP OClW RPB TxU ViU *Great Britain*: BM EU GU OT *USSR*: LL Available from Inter Documentation Company.

Vostochnaia filologiia. Tblisi. 1969– (PJ25.V6) DLC CaQMM ICU NIC *USSR*: LL

Vyzvol'nyi shliakh; suspil'no-politychnyi i naukovo-literaturnyi misiachnyk. London. v. (AP58.U5V9) DLC *Great Britain*: BM LSL

Vznik a počátku Slovanů. Prague. 1, 1956– (D147.V9) DLC ICU NIC NNC Available from Kraus Reprint.

Die Welt der Slaven. Wiesbaden. 1, 1956– (PG1.W4) DLC CSt CU IaU IU NN NNC *Great Britain*: BM C LSL O OT

Wiadomości archeologiczne. Warsaw. 1, 1873– DLC CtY CU NNM *Great Britain*: BM

Wiadomości ludoznawcze. Łódz. 1, 1932– MH NNM

Wiener Slawistischer Almanach. Wien. 1978– (PG1.W53) DLC CLU CSt CtY InU IU KU MiEM NIC NjP NN NNC

Wisła, Warsaw. 1, 1887– (DK401.W55) DLC MH NhD OCl *Great Britain*: BM

Z otchłani wieków. Wrocław. 1, 1926– (DK409.Z2) DLC IEN IU NN NNM

Zbornik za narodni život i običaje južnih slavena. Zagreb. 1, 1896–
(DB369.5Z4) DLC CtY CU IU MH MiU *Great Britain*: BM Available
from Kraus Reprint.

Zeitschrift des Heimatkundes Mecklenburg. Schwerin. 1906–41.

Zeitschrift fuer Archaeologie. Berlin. 1, 1967– DLC CU InU MiU MnU
NjP

Zeitschrift fuer Deutsche Mythologie und Sittenkunde. Goettingen. 1, 1853–
DLC CSt CtY CU ICU IU MB MH NIC NjP NN NNC OCl PU RPB
WU *Great Britain*: BM LUC LWI O *France*: BN S

Zeitschrift fuer die historische Theologie. Leipzig. 1, 1831– (BR140.Z36)
DLC DS ICMcC IEN NUT *Great Britain*: C O *France*: S

Zeitschrift fuer Ethnologie. Berlin. 1, 1869– DLC CLU CSt CtY CU ICN
IEN IU OClW MB MiU WaU *Great Britain*: BM C CH EU GU LAI
OT *France*: BN S US

Zeitschrift fuer Missionskunde und Religionswissenschaft. Berlin. 1, 1886–
(BV3400.Z4) DLC ICU NIC

Zeitschrift fuer slavische Literatur, Kunst und Wissenschaft. Bautzen. 1,
1862– ICN MH NN *Great Britain*: BM O *France*: BN S

Zeitschrift fuer slavische Philologie. Leipzig. 1, 1924– (PG1.Z4) DLC CtY
CU ICN ICU IU MdBJ MH MnU MoU NIC NN NNC OCl OClW
OCU WU *Great Britain*: BM C LdU LSL *France*: BN Available from
Kraus Reprint.

Zeitschrift fuer Slawistik. Berlin. 1, 1956– (PG1.Z43) DLC CaBVaU CaQNU
CtY CU ICU IU MH MiU NIC NNC PU WU *Great Britain*: BM C
LSL O OT

Zeitschrift fuer vergleichende Sprachforschung auf dem Gebiete der indo-
germanischen Sprachen. Berlin. 1, 1852– (P501.Z5) DLC CaOTU CSt
CtY CU IEN IU KU KyU MH MiU MnU NIC NjP NN NNC OCU
RPB WU *Great Britain*: BM *France*: BN Available from Kraus
Reprint.

Zhivaia starina. St. Petersburg. 1, 1890– (GN1.Z5) DLC CtY CU IU MnU
NNC *Great Britain*: BM *USSR*: LL Available from Inter Documentation Company.

Zhurnal dlia chteniia vospitannikam voenno-uchebnykh zavedenii. St.
Petersburg. 1836– DLC CtY *USSR*: LL

Znanie. St. Petersburg. 1, 1870– DLC IU MH NcD NN *USSR*: LL

Inter Documentation Company AG
Poststrasse 14
Zug, Switzerland

Kraus Reprint Company (US Division)
Rte 100
Millwood, New York 10546

University Microfilms International
300 North Zeeb Road
Ann Arbor, Michigan 48106

PRIMARY SOURCES

1. Adamus, Bremenis. *Gesta Hammaburgensis ecclesiae pontificum.* in Monumenta Germaniae Historica inde ad anno Christi quingentesimo usque ad annum millesimum et quingentesimum. *Scriptorum.* Hannoverae, t.7 (1846) pp 267-389. (DD3.M8S4) DLC CaBVaU CU MH MiU MoSU NBuU NcD NcU NjP OCl OkU OrU OU PSt ScU TxHR ViU *Great Britain*: BM *France*: BN

2. Cosmas, of Prague. *Die chronik Boehmen des Cosmas von Prag.* Berlin, Wiedmannsche Buchhandlung, 1923. 295 p. (Series: Monumenta Germaniae Historica inde ad anno Christi quingentesimo usque ad annum millesimu et quingetesium. *Scriptores rerum Germanicarum.* nova ser., t.2) (DDD3.M8S5 t.2) DLC CaBVaU CaOTU CtY CU GU ICN LU MB MH MiU NcD NhD NN OCl OCU OU PU *Great Britain*: BM *France*: BN

3. Ebbo. *Vita Ottonis episcopi Babenbergensis.* in Monumenta Germaniae Historica inde ad anno Christi quingentesimo usque ad annum millesimum et quingentesimum. *Scriptorum.* Hannoverae, t.12 (1856) pp 822-883. (DD3.M8S4) DLC CaBVaU CU MH MiU MoSU NBuU NcD NcU NjP OCl OkU OrU OU PSt ScU TxHR ViU *Great Britain*: BM *France*: BN

4. Harkavi, A. Ia. *Skazaniia musulmanskikh pisatelei o slavianakh i russkikh s poloviny VII veka do kontsa X veka.* St. Petersburg, 1870. 308 p. (D90.S5 no.3) Also 1969 reprint, The Hague, Mouton, Slavistic printings and reprintings, no.96. DLC AkU CaBVaU CaOTU CaQMM CLSU CLU CNoS CoU CSt CtY CU CU-S CU-SC DDO GU IaU ICU IEdS IEN InU IU KyU LU MdU MH MiU MnU MU MWelC NcD NcU NhD NIC NjR NN NNC NSyU OrCS OrPS OrU OU PPiU RPB TNJ TU TxHR TxU UU ViU WaU WU *Great Britain*: BM *USSR*: GPIB LL (Tales of Moslem writers concerning the Slavs and Russians from the mid 7th century to the end of the 10th century)

5. Helmoldus. *Helmoldi presbyteri bosoviensis Cronica Slavorum.* Hannoverae et Lipsiae, Impensis Bibliopolii, Hahniani, 1909. 273 p. (DD3.M82) DLC CtY CU NIC NN OCl PBm

6. Herbordus. *Herbordi dialogus de vita Ottonis episcopi Babenbergensis.* Hannoverae, Impensis Bibliopolii, Hahniani, 1868. 166 p. (DD3.M82) DLC CtY CU MH NN OClW

7. Iatsimirskii, A. I. *Khristomatiia po slavianskim drevnostiiam. Verova-niia.* Rostov na Donu, 1916. 96 p. *USSR:* LL (A reader on Slavic antiquities. Belief)

8. *Knytlinga Saga.* in *Fornmanna Soeger.* Kjøbenhavn, Popp, v.11 (1828) pp 179-402. (PT7260.F6A1 1825) DLC CU MdBP NIC OCl

9. Meyer, Karl Heinrich. *Fontes historiae religionis slavicae.* Berolini, Apud Walter de Gruyter et socios, 1931. 112 p. (Series: Fontes historiae religionum ex auctoribus graecis et latinis collectos edidit Carolus Clemen, fasciculus IV) (BL74.F6 fasc 4) DLC CaBVaU CtY CtY-D CU DDO IaU MH MiU NcD NN OCl OClW RPB TNJ-R *Great Britain:* BM

10. Monachus Priflingensis. *Vita Ottonis episcopi.* in Monumenta Germaniae Historica inde ad anno Christi quingetesimo usque ad annum illesimum et quingetesimum. *Scriptorum.* Hannoverae, t.12 (1856) pp 883-903. (DD3.M8S4) DLC CaBVaU CU MH MiU MoSU NBuU NcD NcU NjP OCl OkU OrU OU PSt ScU TxHR ViU *Great Britain:* BM *France:* BN

11. *Povest' vremennykh let.* in *Lavrent'evskaia letopis'.* Leningrad, ANSSSR, 1926. 286 p. (Series: Akademiia nauk SSSR. Arkheologicheskaia komissiia. *Polnoe sobranie russkikh letopisei,* t.1, vyp.1) Exists in various editions. (DK70.A53) DLC CaOTU CLU GU InU NcD NcU NIC NjP NN OkU OU TxHR WU *Great Britain:* BM *USSR:* GPIB LL (Tale of bygone years)

12. Procopius, of Caesarea. *Procopii Caesariensis opera omnia.* Lipsiae, 1905-13. 3v. in 4. Exists in various editions. (PA3404.P85 1905) DLC CSt CU DDO MiU NjP

13. Saxo Grammaticus. *Saxonis gesta danorum.* Haunie, 1931- (DL147.S27 1931) DLC CtY CU DDO GU InU KU LU MoSU NcD NIC NN OCl OrU OU PU TU TxU ViU WaU

14. *Slovo o polku Igoreve.* V.P. Adrianova-Peretts, ed. Moskva, Izd-vo Akademii nauk SSSR, 1950. 483 p. Exists in various editions. (PG3300.S6 1950) DLC CaOTU CtY CU ICU MdBJ MH NBC NIC NjP *USSR:* GPIB LL (The song of Igor's campaign)

15. Thietmar. *Thietmari Chronicon.* in Monumenta Germaniae Historica inde ad anno Christi quingentesimo usque ad anum millesimum et quingentesimum. *Scriptorum.* Hannoverae, t.3 (1839) pp 723-871. (DD3.M8S4) DLC CaBVaU CU MH MiU MoSU NBuU NcD NcU NjP OCl OkU OrU OU PSt ScU TxHR ViU *Great Britain:* BM *France:* BN

16.   Znayenko, Myroslava T. [Selections from sources] in her *The gods of*
       the ancient Slavs. Tatishchev and the beginnings of Slavic mythol-
       ogy. Columbus, Slavica, 1980. pp 181-216. DLC AU AzTeS AzU
       CoU InU KyU OKentU OkU OOxM OU PPiU PPT ViBlbV
       WaU WU

SECONDARY SOURCES

17. Afanas'ev, Aleksandr Nikolaevich. "Iazycheskiia predaniia ob ostrov Buian." in Moscow. Universitet. Obshchestvo istorii i drevnostei rossiskikh. *Vremennik*, 1851, kn.9, pp 1-24. (Pagan legends concerning the island of Buian)

18. Afanas'ev, Aleksandr Nikolaevich. *Poeticheskiia vozzreniia slavian na prirodu.* St. Petersburg, Izd. K. Soldatenkova, 1865-69, 3v. (BL310.A4) Also 1969 reprint, The Hague, Mouton, Slavistic printings and reprintings, no. 214. Available from University Microfilms International. DLC CaBVaU CaOTU CLSU CoU CSt CtW CU-SB CU-SC FTaSU GU IaU IEdS IEN InU KU KyU LU MeB MH MiEM MiU MnU NhD NIC NjP NjR NNC NSyU RPB TNJ TxHR TxU ViU WaU *Great Britain*: BM *USSR*: BAN GPIB LL (The poetic views of the Slavs toward nature)

19. Agrell, Sigurd. *Slaviska myter och sagor.* Stockholm, Bokfoerlaget Natur och Kultur, 1929. 240 p. ICU NN

20. Aigner, P. "O świątyniach u starożytnych i o Słowiańskich." in Towarzystwo warszawskie przyjaciol nauk. *Rocznik*, 7 (1811) pp 293-311. (Concerning temples, antiquities and the Slavs)

21. Albrecht, C. "Slavische Bildwerke," *Mainzer Zeitschrift*, 23 (1928) pp 46-52.

22. Alexinsky, G. "Mythologie slave." in Guirand, Felix. *Mythologie générale.* Paris, Larousse, 1935. pp 253-69. (BL310.G85) DLC CoU GU IaU N NcGU OClMA OO PBm TxU WaS

23. Alexinsky, G. "Slavic mythology." in *Larousse Encyclopedia of Mythology.* New York, Prometheus Press, 1959, pp 293-310. (BL310.L453) DLC AAP CaBVaU CLU CSt CU DSI FTaSU FU GAT GEU GU IaU InU IU KU KyU MB MH MiU MoSU MtU NcD NIC NjP NjR NN NNC NRU OCl OClW OCU OkU OO OOxM OrCS OrU OU PBm PP RPB ScU TNJ TxU ViU WaU WU

24. Andjelić, P. "Srednjevekovna kultna mjesta u okoliny Konjica," Sarajevo. Zemaljski muzej. *Glasnik*, 12 (1957) pp 185-99. (Medieval cult places in the vicinity of Konjic)

25. Anichkov, Evgenii Vasil'evich. *Iazychestvo i drevniaia Rus'*. Petrograd, Tip. M.M. Stasiulevicha, 1914. 386 p. (Series: Leningrad. Universitet. Istoriko-filologicheskii fakul'tet. *Zapiski*, chast' 117) (AS262.L4223) DLC CSt IU MiU NcU RPB ViU WaU *USSR*: BAN GPIB LL (Paganism and ancient Rus)

26. Anichkov, Evgenii Vasil'evich. "Narodnaia poeziia i drevniaia verovaniia slavian." in his *Istoriia russkoi literatury*. Moskva, Izd. T-va N.D. Sytina, 1908, pp 43-80. (PG2950.A6) DLC CLU CtY CU ICU InU IU MiU MnU NcD NIC NN OCl OU RPB ViU WaU WU *Great Britain*: BM *USSR*: LL (Folk poetry and the ancient beliefs of the Slavs)

27. Anichkov, Evgenii Vasil'evich. "Old Russian pagan cults." in International Congress for the History of Religions, 3rd., Oxford, 1908. *Transactions*, v.2, pp 244-60 (BL21.I6 1908) DLC CaBVaU CtY IaU MB MH MiU NcD NIC OrU *Great Britain*: BM

28. Anichkov, Evgenii Vasil'evich. "Posledniia raboty po slavianskim religioznym drevnostiiam," *Slavia*, 2 (1923-24) pp 527-47. (The latest works on Slavic religious antiquities)

29. Antoniewicz, Włodzimierz. "O religii dawnych Słowian," *Światowit*, 20 (1948-49) pp 327-44. French summary. (Concerning the religion of the ancient Slavs)

30. Antoniewicz, Włodzimierz. "Religia dawnych Słowian." in *Religie świata*. Warszawa, Instytut Wydawniczy Pax, 1958. pp 319-402. *USSR*: ANSSSR–INION Reviewed in *Przegląd historyczny*, 50 (1959) no. 2, pp 127-30. (The religion of the ancient Slavs)

31. Arendt, Martin Friedrich. *Grossherzolich-strelitzisches Georgium nord-slavischer Gottheiten und ihre Dienstes*. Minden, Boesendahl, 1820. 7 p. MB

32. "Arkona," *Przyjaciel ludzi*, 25 (1837) pp 196-7.

33. Arnkiel, Trogillus. *M. Trogilli Arnkiels . . . Aussfuehrliche Eroeffnung/ . . . Was es mit der cimbrischen und mitternaechtischen Voelcker als Sachsen/Gothen/Wenden und Fresen ihrem Goetzendienst/ Hayden/Oraculen/Zaubereyen/Begraebnissen u.d.gl. von uhralters her vor eine Bewandtniss gehabt . . .* Hamburg, T. von Wiering, 1703. 4 parts. Exists in various editions. CtY CU ICU MH NIC NjP NN PPULC PU *Great Britain*: BM *France*: BN *USSR*: LL

34. Ayrer, Georg Heinrich. *Hermannus Slavicus*. Goettingen, Sumtibus V. Bossiegel, 1768. 128 p. *Great Britain*: BM *France*: BN

35.   Azbukin, M. "Ocherk literaturnoi bor'by predstavitelei khristianstva s ostatkami iazychestva v russkom narode XI–XIV v," *Russkii filologicheskii vestnik.* 28 (1892) no.3, pp 133-53, 36 (1896) no.2, pp 221-72, 39 (1898) nos.1-2, pp 246-76. (An essay on the literary struggle of the representatives of Christianity with the remnants of paganism in the Russian people from the 11th to the 14th centuries)

36.   Babagiolo, Mario. *Credenze religiose degli Slavi precristiani.* n.p., Centro studi Russia Cristiana, 1968. 222 p. (BL930.B3) DLC DDO NIC NjP

37.   Baiburin, A. "K vostochnoslavianskim dannym o Svaroge," *Slavica hierosolymitana*, 5-6 (1981) pp 57-60. (Eastern Slavic information on Svarog)

38.   Bandtke, J. S. "O iazycheskoi religii drevnei Pol'shi," *Vestnik Evropy*, 1826, ch. 145, no.3, p 207, no.4, p 253. (Concerning the pagan religion of ancient Poland)

39.   Baskakov, N. A. "Mifologicheskie i epicheskie imena sobstvennye v "Slove o polku Igoreve" (K etimologii "Veles" i "Boian")," *Vostochnaia filologiia*, 1973, no.3, pp 183-92. French summary. (The mythological and epic proper names in the Slovo o polku Igoreve (concerning the etymology of Veles and Boian))

40.   Becker, J. "Faelschung und Betrug in der vorgeschichte Mecklenburgs," *Mecklenburgische Monatshefte*, 12 (1936) pp 224-8.

41.   Beckmann, P. "Die Rethra-Sagen in Mecklenburg," *Deutsches Jahrbuch fuer Volkskunde*, 5 (1959) no.1, pp 44-73.

42.   Beilis, V. M. "K otsenke svedenii arabskikh avtorov o religii drevnikh slavian i rusov." in Tveritinova, Anna Stepanovna. *Vostochnye istochniki po istorii narodov iugo-vostochnoi i tsentral'oi Evropy.* Moskva, Nauka, 1974. pp 72-89. (DR1.T9) DLC CaBVaU CaOTU CLSU CSt CtY CU CU-SB FMU GU IaU ICU InU IU KU MB MH MiEM MiU MnU MoU NcD NcU NIC NjP NN NNC NSyU OrU OU PPiU RPB TNJ TxU ViU WaU WU *USSR*: GPIB LL (An appraisal of the data of Arab authors concerning the religion of the ancient Slavs and Rus)

43.   Bender, Witold. "Bogowie i uczeni," *Z otchłani wieków*, 44 (1978) no.4, pp 243-4. (Gods and scholars)

44.   Beranová, M. "K otázce vícehlavosti slovanských bohů," *Archeologické rozhledy*, 7 (1955) no.6, pp 804-8. French and Russian summaries. (Concerning the polycephalous nature of the Slavic gods)

45. Berezin, L. "O mifologicheskikh verovaniiakh avstriiskikh iuzhnykh slavian," *Znanie*, 1877, no.3, pp 1-34, no.4, pp 51-84. (Concerning the mythological beliefs of the Austrian southern Slavs)

46. Berlekamp, Hansdieter. "Badania grodu Światowita," *Z otchłani wieków*, 37 (1971) no.4, pp 269-71. (Research on Światowit's town)

47. Berneker, Erich Karl. "Ein slavischer Goettername." in *Aufsaetz zur Kultur- und Sprachgeschichte vornehmlich des Orients*. Breslau, M & H Marcus, 1916. pp 176-83. CU ICN ICU IU MH NcU NjP NN PPULC WU

48. Bernhardy, W. "Bausteine zur slawischen Mythologie," *Jahrbuecher fuer slawische Literatur, Kunst und Wissenschaft*, 1 (1843) H.5, pp 336-44, H.6, pp 383-408, 3 (1844) H.1, pp 21-8.

49. Beseliev, I. "Grucki i latinski izvori za vjarata na prabulgarite," Sofia. Naroden etnografski muzei. *Izvestiia*, 8-9 (1929), pp 149-92. (Greek and Latin sources for the beliefs of the proto-Bulgarians)

50. Beyer, W. G. "Die Hauptgottheiten der westwendische Voelkerschaften," *Mecklenburgische Jahrbuecher*, 37 (1873), pp 115-69.

51. Beyer, W. G. "Die Landwehren und die Grenz-Heiligthuemer des Landes der Redarier," *Mecklenburgische Jahrbuecher*, 37 (1872) pp 42-114.

52. Beyer, W. G. "Ueber ein parchimisches Goetzenbilt," *Mecklenburgische Jahrbuecher*, 8 (1843) pp 151-3.

53. Beyer, W. G. "Die wendische Schwerine. Ein Beitrag zur Erlaeuterung des slavischen Goetzendienstes," *Mecklenburgische Jahrbuecher*, 32 (1867) pp 58-148.

54. "Ein Beytrag zur aelteren Geschichte Mecklenburgs und besonders ueber die Lage der Stadt Rethra und des Tempels des Radegast," *Monatsschrift von und fuer Mecklenburg*, 3 (1790) pp 99-114, 225-38.

55. Bezlaj, Francè. "Nekaj besedi o slovenski mitologiji v zadnjih desetih letih," *Slovenski Etnograf*, 3-4 (1950-51) pp 342-53. French summary. (A few words on Slavic mythology in the last ten years)

56. Birnbaum, Henrik. "Der oesterreichische Jasomirgott und das Problem der fruehesten Ausbreitung der Alpenslaven (Urslovenen)," *Anzeiger fuer Slavische Philologie*, 9 (1977) pp 33-48. See no. 57

57.   Birnbaum, Henrik. "Der oesterreichische Jasomirgott und das Problem der fruehesten Ausbreitung der Alpenslaven (Urslovenen)." in his *Essays in early Slavic civilization.* Munich, Wilhelm Fink Verlag, 1981, pp 66-81. IaU NIC NjP NN RPB See no. 56

58.   Blankoff, Jean. "Deux survivances du paganisme en vielle Russie: 1. Les ornaments en croissants de lune, 2. Le culte de l'ours," *Slavica Gandensia*, 7-8 (1980-81) pp 215-49, 13 (1981) pp 9-29.

59.   Bodianskii, Osip Maksimovich. "Ob odnom prologie Moskovskoi dukhovnoi tipografii i tozhdestvie slavianskikh bozhestv, khorsa i dazhd'boga," Moscow. Universitet. Obshchestvo istorii i drevnostei rossiskikh. *Chteniia*, (1846) otd.1 (ch.2), pp 5-23. (Concerning a prologue of the Moscow Ecclesiastical printer and the identities of the Slavic gods Khors and Dazhbog) See no. 60

60.   Bodianskii, Osip Maksimovich. *Ob odnom prologie Moskovskoi Dukhovnoi Tipografii i tozhdestvie slavisnskikh bozhestv, Khorsa i Dazhd'boga.* Moskva, Univ. Tip. 1846. 23 p. *USSR*: LL (Concerning a prologue of the Moscow Ecclesiastical Printer and the identities of the Slavic gods, Khors and Dazhbog) See no. 59

61.   Bogatyrev, Petr Grigor'evich. *Actes magiques; rites et croyances en Russie subcarpathique.* Paris, H. Champion, 1929. 162 p. (Series: Travaux publiés par L'Institut d'Etudes Slaves, 11) DLC-P4 CU ICU IEN MH MiU NcD NIC NjP NjR NN NNC NSyU OCl OrU OU PPULC PU WaU *Great Britain*: BM

62.   Boguslawski, Wilhelm. "Pogaństwo." in his *Dzieje Słowiańszczyzny połnoco-zachodniej do połowiny XIII w.* Poznan, Nakł. Autora, 1889-1900. v.2, section 2, chap 27, pp 710-862. (D147.B65) DLC ICU MH N NNC WaU *Great Britain*: BM (Paganism)

63.   Boldur, A. "Iaroslavna i russkoe dvoeverie v "Slove o polku Igoreve," *Russkaia literatura*, 1964, no.1, pp 84-6. (The reign of Iaroslav and Russian dual faith in the Slovo o polku Igoreve)

64.   Boldur, A. "Troian Slova o polku Igoreve." in Akademiia nauk SSSR. Institut russkoi literatury. Otdel drevnerusskoi literatury. *Trudy*, 15 (1958) pp 7-35. (Troian of the Slovo o polku Igoreve)

65.   Boll, Franz Christian. "Kritische Geschichte der sogenannten Prillwitzer Idole," *Mecklenburgische Jahrbuecher*, 19 (1854) pp 162-286.

66.   Boll, Franz Christian. "Nachtrag zu den kritischen Geschichte der sogenannten "Prillwitzer Idole," *Mecklenburgische Jahrbuecher*, 20 (1855) pp 208-27.

67. Boll, Franz Christian. "Ueber die Lage von Rhetra bei Prilwitz und ueber die sogenannten Prilwitzer Idole," *Archiv fuer Landeskunde*, 1853, pp 40-69.

68. Boll, Franz Christian. "Ueber die sog. Prilwitzer Idole im grossh. Altertums-Cabinet zu Neustrelitz." in his *Chronik der Vorderstadt Neubrandenburg*. Neubrandenburg, 1875. Anhang 1, pp 279-300. *Great Britain*: BM

69. Bolsunovskii, Karl Vasil'evich. *Pamiatniki slavianskoi mifologii*. Kiev, Tip.-Lit. S.V. Kul'zhenko, 1914. 17 p. *USSR*: GPIB LL (Relics of Slavic mythology)

70. Bolsunovskii, Karl Vasil'evich. *Ślady obrządow pogańskikh na ziemach słowian*. Kiev, Tip. Tov. E.A. Sin'kevich, 1913. 10 p. *USSR*: LL (The traces of pagan rites in Slavic lands)

71. Bolsunovskii, Karl Vasil'evich. *Zhertvennik Germesa-Svietovida*. Kiev, Tip. T-va G.L. Frontskevicha i Ko, 1909. 18 p. IU *USSR*: LL (The altar of Hermes-Swiatowit)

72. Borchling, C. "Aus der slawischen Mythologie," *Praehistorische Zeitschrift*, 11 (1909) pp 171-9.

73. Borovskii, Iaroslav Evgen'evich. *Mifologicheskii mir drevnikh kievlian*. Kiev, Naukova Dumka, 1982. 103 p. (BL930.B65 1982) DLC AzTeS CU-SB GU InU IU MiEM OrU (The mythological world of the ancient Kievans)

74. "Bóstwo słońca, Światowid," *Magazyn powszechny*, 1834, no.3, p 345. (The god of the sun, Swiatowit)

75. Braichevskii, M. IU. & Dovzhenok, V. I. "Drevneslavianskoe sviatilishche v s. Ivankovtsy na Podnestrov'e." in Akademiia nauk URSR, Kiev. Instytut arkheologii. *Kratkie soobshcheniia*, vyp. 2 (1953) pp 23-4. (An ancient Slavic sanctuary in the village of Ivankovtsa on the Dnester)

76. Braichevskii, M. IU. "Drevneslavianskoe sviatilishche v sele Ivankovtsy na Dnestre," Akademiia nauk SSSR. Institut arkheologii. *Kratkie soobshcheniia o dokladakh i polevykh issledovaniiakh*, 52 (1953) pp 43-53. (An ancient Slavic sanctuary in the village of Ivankovtsa on the Dnestr)

77. Braichevskii, M. IU. & Dovzhenok, V. I. "Poselenie i sviatilishche v sele Ivankovtsy v srednem Podnestrov'e." in *Istoriia i arkheologiia iugo-zapadnykh oblastei SSSR nachala nashei ery*. B.A. Rybakov & E.A. Symonovich, eds. Moskva, Nauka, 1967. pp

238-62. (GN824.U6I8) DLC CLU CSt CU DDO IaU MH MiU MU NcU NIC NSyU OrU RPB ViU *USSR*: GPIB LL (The settlement and sanctuary in the village of Ivankovtsa on the middle Dnestr)

78. Brandl, V. "Příspěvek k mythologii česke," Matice Moravska, Bruenn. *Sbornik*, 8 (1876) pp 59-76. (A contribution to Czech mythology)

79. Bronisch, W. "Etymologischer Versuch ueber den Namen Flyns," *Neues Lausitzisches Magazin*, 21 (1843) pp 218-29.

80. Brueckner, Alexander. "Fantazje mitologiczne," *Slavia*, 8 (1929-30) pp 34-51. (Mythological imagination)

81. Brueckner, Alexander. *Mitologia slava*. Bologna, N. Zanicelli, 1923. 282 p. (BL930.B68) DLC ICU MH NcD NN PP PPULC

82. Brueckner, Alexander. *Mitologia słowiańska i polska*. Warszawa, Państwowe Wydawnictwo Naukowe, 1980. 383 p. (BL930.B78) DLC InU KU NBuU OU ViU (Slavic and Polish mythology)

83. Brueckner, Alexander. *Mitologja polska*. Warszawa, Instytut Wydawniczy "Bibljoteka polska", 1924. 144 p. ICU MH MiD MiU NB NN OCl PCamA PPULC WU (Polish mythology)

84. Brueckner, Alexander. *Mitologja słowiańska*. Krakow, Nakł. Akademji Umiejętności, 1918. 152 p. (BL30.B68) DLC-P4 CSt CtY ICU MH MiDW MiU PPULC PU Reviewed in *Slavia*, 2 (1923-240 pp 527-47, 765-78. (Slavic mythology)

85. Brueckner, Alexander. "Mythologische Studien," *Archiv fuer slavische Philologie*, 15 (1892) pp 161-91.

86. Brueckner, Alexander. "Mythologische Thesen," *Archiv fuer slavische Philologie*, 40 (1925) pp 1-21.

87. Brueckner, Alexander. "O paganstvu kod starikh Slovena," *Knjiga o Balkanu*, 2 (1937) pp 51-61. (Concerning paganism among the old Slavs)

88. Brueckner, Alexander. "Oesteuropaische Goetternamen," *Zeitschrift fuer vergleichende Sprachforschung auf dem Gebiete der indogermanischen Sprachen*, 50 (1922) pp 161-97.

89. Brueckner, Alexander. "Pierwotna wiara i kulty." in *Polska, jej dzieje i kultura od czasów najdawniejszych do chwili obecej*. Warszawa, Nakł. Trzaski, Everta i Michalskiego, 1927-32. v.1, H.2-3, pp 39-50. (DK414.P84) DLC CoU CSt CtY IU NcU NN NNC ViU (Primitive beliefs and cults)

90. Brueckner, Alexander. "Pripegala," *Archiv fuer slavische Philologie*, 6 (1882) pp 216-23.

91. Brueckner, Alexander. *Die Slaven*. Tuebingen, Mohr, 1926 43 p. (Series: Religionsgeschichtliches Lebensbuch, 2, Erweiterte Aufl. 3) (BL25.R381 1926 no.3) DLC DDO ICU MH MiU MoU NcD NIC OCl *Federal Republic of Germany*: JGH

92. Brueckner, Alexander. "Slaven und Litauer," in Chantepie de la Saussaye, Pierre Daniel. *Lehrbuch der Religionsgeschichte*. Tuebingen, Mohr, 1925. pp 506-29. (BL80.C34 1925) DLC CSt CtY CU MH MiU NcD NIC OClW OCU OU PSt RPB TNJ-R Exists in numerous editions.

93. Brueckner, Alexander. "Zur Geschichte des Aberglaubens in Polen," *Archiv fuer slavische Philologie*, 15 (1893) pp 316-7.

94. Buchholtz, Samuel. *Rhetra und dessen Goetzen*. Buetzow und Wismar, 1773. 58 p. *Great Britain*: BM

95. Buchholtz, Samuel. "Rhetra und dessen Goetzen." in Masch, Andreas Gottlieb. *Beytraege zur Erlaeuterung der obotritischen Alterthuemer*, Schwerin und Guestrow, Buchenrieder und Ritter, 1774. pp 61-74. *Great Britain*: BM *USSR*: LL

96. Budde, V. S. "Mificheskii element v russkoi narodnoi slovesnosti," *Filologicheskiia zapiski*, 1883, vyp. 5-6, pp 1-37. (The mythical element in Russian folklore)

97. Buelow, C. C. "Ueber die wendischen Schwerine," *Mecklenburgische Jahrbuecher*, 34 (1869) pp 191-5.

98. Buesching, Johann Gustav Gottlieb. *Das Bild des Gottes fyr, gefunden in Oberschlesien und verglichen mit zwei andern bildern desselben gottes, entdeckt am Rhein und in Meklenburg*. Breslau, 1819. 22 p. MH RPB

99. Bukowski, Serge. "Mythes slaves et finnois." in *L'Europe paienne: Grecs, Romains, Celtes, Scandinaves, Germains, Slaves*. de Smedt, Marc, ed. Paris, Seghers, 1979. pp 215-241 (BL690.E95) DLC AzTeS CU-SB IU MH ViBlbV WaU

100. Bukowski, Stanisław. "Świątynia Światowida — jak mogła wyglądać," *Z otchłani wieków*, 40 (1974) no.1, pp 76-8. (The temple of Swiatowit — how it looked)

101. Bulakhovs'kyi, Leonid Arsen'evich. "Lingvistychni uvahy mifolohichni nazvy "Slova o polku Ihorevie," *Movoznavstvo*, 15 (1959) pp 21-32. (Linguistic considerations concerning the mythological names of the Slovo o polku Igoreve) See no. 102

102. Bulakhovs'kyi, Leonid Arsen'evich. "Lingvistychni uvahy mifolo-hichni nazvy "Slova o polku Ihorevie." in his *Vybrani pratsi.* Kiev, Naukova Dumka, v.3 (1978) pp 494-507. (PG15.B8 1975) DLC CLU NIC OU UU WU *USSR*: LL (Linguistic considerations concerning the mythological names of the Slovo o polku Igoreve) See no. 101

103. Buschan, G. "Das Rethra-Heiligtum," *Unser Pommerland,* 1 (1912-13) pp 7-9.

104. Cabalska, M. "Aus den Studien ueber die Religion der heidnischen Slawen." in Congrès International d'Archéologie Slave. 3rd., Bratislava, 1975. *Rapports,* v.1, pp 125-40. DLC AAP DDO InU NcU OU TxU ViU WaU

105. Cabalska, M. "Ze studiów nad religia pogańskich Słowian," Polska Akademia Nauk. Oddział w Krakowie. *Sprawozdania,* 16 (1972) cz.1, pp 7-8. (From research on the pagan religion of the Slavs)

106. Cabalska, M. "Ze studiów nad religia pogańskich Słowian," Krakow. Muzeum archeologiczne. *Materiały archeologiczne,* 14 (1973) pp 103-31. (From research on the pagan religion of the Slavs)

107. Čajkanovic, Veselin. *O srpskom vrhovnom bogu.* Beograd, 1941. 208 p. (Series: Srpska akademija nauk, Belgrad. Posebna izdanja, knj. 132) (AS346.B53 no. 132) DLC CaBVaU CoU CSt DDO IU KU NIC NN OCl OrU OU *USSR*: GPIB (Concerning the highest god of the Serbs)

108. Čajkanovic, Veselin. "O vrkhovnom bogu u staroi srpskoj religiji." in his *Mit i religija u Srba. Izabranje studije.* Beograd, Srpska knjizevna zadruga, 1973. pp 307-462. (Series: Srpska knjizevna zadruga. Izdanja, kolo 66, knj. 443) (BL980.S6C3) DLC FTaSU InU MH MiEM MiU NNC TNJ ViU WaU *USSR*: GPIB (Concerning the highest god in the old Serbian religion)

109. Camozzini, M. "La religioni dei Celti, dei Germani e degli Slavi." in Turchi, Nicola. *Le Religioni del mondo.* Roma, Coletti, 1951. 719 p. DLC

110. Carriere, Moriz. "Die Mythologie und Volkspoesie der Slawen," *Internationale Revue,* 1 (1866) no.2, pp 177-91, no.3, pp 372-81.

111. Cehak-Hołubowicza, Helena. "Badania nad wierzeniami religijnymi w starożytnosci i wczesnym średniowieczu na terenie Śląska." in *Religia pogańskich Słowian; sesja naukowa w Kielcach.* Kielce, 1968. pp 69-80. (Studies on religious beliefs on the territory of Silesia in antiquity and the early Middle Ages) See no. 635

112. Cehak-Hołubowicza, Helena. "Kamienne konstrukcje kultowe pod szczytem na północnym stoku góry Ślęży," *Światowit*, 23 (1960) pp 479-92. (Stone cult structures under the peak, on the northern slope of Sleza mountain)

113. Cehak-Hołubowicza, Helena. "Kamienne kregi kultowe na Raduni i Ślęży," *Archeologia Polski*, 3 (1959) z.1, pp 51-97. German summary. (Stone cult circles on the Radun and Sleza)

114. Cehak-Hołubowicza, Helena. "Odkrycia zwiazane z kultem pogańskim na Śląsku we wczesnym średniowieczu." in *Congres International d'Archeologie Slave*. 1st., Warsaw, 1965. Wrocław, Zakład Narodowy im. Ossolińskich, v.5 (1968) pp 393-406. French summary. (GN700.C58 1965) DLC CaBVaU CaOTP CaQMM CLU CoU CSt CtY CU DDO DSI FU IaU ICU InNd InU IU MH MH-P MiU MnU MoU MU NcD NcU NjP NN NNC OU TxU (Discoveries connected with pagan cults in Silesia in the early Middle Ages)

115. Cehak-Hołubowicza, Helena. "Olimp śląska." in Maleczynska, Ewa. *Szkice z dziejów Śląka*. Warszawa, Ksiąska i Wiedza, 1955. T.1, pp 1-19. (DD491.S422M3) DLC IU (The Silesian Olympus)

116. Cehak-Hołubowicza, Helena. "Relikty pogańskich religijnow." in Polska Akademia Nauk. Instytut historii kultury materialnej. *Pierwsza sesja archeologiczna Instytutu Historii Kultury Materialniej Polskiej Akademii Nauk*, Warsaw., 1955. Warszawa, Wydawn. Polskiej Akademii Nauk, 1957. pp 376-7. CU InU MiDW (Relics of pagan religions)

117. Černý, Adolf. "Istoty mityczne Serbów łużyckich," *Wisła*, 12 (1898) p 673. (Mythical beings of the Lusatian Sorbs)

118. Černý, Adolf. *Istoty mityczne Serbów łużyckich*. Warszawa, Drukarina Rebieszewskiego i Wrotnowskiego, 1901. 444 p. *USSR*: LL (Mythical beings of the Lusatian Sorbs)

119. Černý, Adolf. "Mythiske bytoscé łužiskich Serbow," Prague. Národní museum. *Časopis*, 43 (1890) pp 3-50, 44 (1891) pp 3-68, 81-129, 45 (1892) pp 25-41, 73-130, 46 (1893) pp 51-67, 47 (1894) pp 76-127, 48 (1895) pp 8-32, 122-44, 49 (1896) pp 3-12, 50 (1897) pp 3-44, 81-118. (Mythical beings of the Lusatian Sorbs) See no. 120

120. Černý, Adolf. *Mythiske bytoscé łužiskich Serbow*. Budyšin, Z nakładom M. Hornika, 1893-98. 2v. (BL980.S6C4) DLC CU NN OCl *Great Britain*: BM Reviewed in *Kwartalnik historiczny*, 13 (1899) p 84. (Mythical beings of the Lusatian Sorbs) See no. 119

121. Černý, Adolf. "Mythiske bytosche łužiskich Serbow," in *Adolf Cerny. Antologija jeho dzěłow*. Budyšin, Domowina, 1958. pp 67-79. (Series: Spisy Instituta za Serbski Ludospyt, 9) (DD491.L322C4) DLC CLU CoU CtY CU ICU InU IU MiDW NBuU NIC NjP NNC (Mythical beings of the Lusatian Sorbs)

122. Chadwick, Nora Kershaw. "The treaties with the Greek and Russian heathenism." in her *The Beginning of Russian history*. Cambridge, The University Press, 1946. pp 76-97 (DK70.A1C5) DLC CaB-VaU CoU CtY CU DDO GU IU KU MB MiU MU NcD NcU NIC OrU OU ViU Reprinted 1977.

123. Chebaev, O. "K voprosu o Troiane v "Slove o polku Igoreve," Alma Ata. Universitet. *Sbornik studencheskikh nauchnykh rabot*, 1972, pp 137-42. (Concerning Troian in Slovo o polku Igoreve)

124. Chernetsov, A. V. "Medieval Russian pictorial materials on paganism and superstitions," *Slavica Gandensia*, 7-8 (1980-81) pp 99-112.

125. Chetyrkin, I. D. "Dva slova o sushchestvovanii idolov u vostochnikh slavian," *Filologicheskiia zapiski*, 1881, vyp.2, pp 9-12. (A few words on the existence of idols among the eastern Slavs)

126. Chlenov, A. M. "Shestibozhzhia kniazia Volodimira," *Ukrains'kyi istorychnyi zhurnal*, 1971, no.8, pp 109-12, no.9, pp 109-12, no.10, pp 114-7. (The six gods of Prince Vladimir)

127. Chodźko, Aleksandr Borejko. *Etudes bulgares*. Etude 1: *Mythologie des chants, slaves du mont rhodope*. Paris, E. Leroux, 1875. 48 p. NIC OCl *Great Britain*: BM *France*: BN

128. Chornii, S. "Kul't sontsa v ukrains'kikh narodnykh viruvanniakh," *Vyzvol'nyi shliiakh*, 33 (1980), no.9, pp 1139-45. (The sun cult in Ukrainian folk belief)

129. Chulkov, Mikhail Dmitrievich. *Abevega ruskikh sueverii, idolopoklon-nicheskikh zhertvoprinoshenii, svadebnykh prostonarodnykh obria-dov, koldostva, shemanstva*. Moskva, 1786. 326 p. MH MiU NN *USSR*: BAN GPIB LL MGU SS (ABC of Russian superstitions, idolatrous sacrifices, folk wedding customs, sorcery, shamanism)

130. Chulkov, Mikhail Dmitrievich. *Slovar' russkikh sueverii*. St. Petersburg, V tip. U Shnora, 1782. 271 p. Also 1786 ed. (GR190.C49 1782) DLC CoU IU NIC NN OCl *Great Britain*: BM *USSR*: BAN GPIB LL MGU SS (A dictionary of Russian superstitions)

131. Clemen, Carl Christian. "Die Religion der Balten und Slaven," *Zeitschrift fuer Missionskunde und Religionswissenschaft*, 53 (1938) pp 76-95.

132. Crepajac, L. "Zum slav. Stribog," *Die Welt der Slaven*, 12 (1967) no. 1, pp 19-21.

133. Curtin, Jeremiah. *Myths and Folk-Tales of the Russians, Western Slavs and Magyars.* Boston, Little, Brown & Co., 1890. 555 p. Exists in various editions. (GR136.C7) DLC CU MH NIC NN OCU WaU *Great Britain*: BM *France*: BN

134. Czajka, H. "Zur Mythologie der Slawen," *Zeitschrift fuer Slawistik*, 25 (1980) no. 2, pp 227-31.

135. Darkevich, V. P. "Topor kak simvol Peruna v drevnerusskom iazychestve," *Sovetskaia arkheologiia*, 5 (1961) no. 4, pp 91-102. (The axe as a symbol of Perun in ancient Russian paganism)

136. Dashkevich, Nikolai Pavlovich. *Slavianorusskii Troian i rimskii imperator Traian.* Kiev, Tip. T. G. Meinandera, 1908. 32 p. IU *USSR*: LL (Slavo-Russian Troian and the Roman emperor Trajan) See no. 137

137. Dashkevich, Nikolai Pavlovich. "Slavianorusskii Troian i rimskii imperator Traian." in *Serta Borysthenica; sbornik v chest' zasluzhennago Profesora imp. un-ta sv. Vladimira Iuliana Andreevicha Kulakovskago.* Kiev, 1911. pp 217-48. IU NIC *USSR*: LL Reprint available from University Microfilms International. (Slavo-Russian Troian and the Roman emperor Trajan) See no. 136

138. Demetrykiewicz, W. "Altertuemliche steinerne, sog. "baby" . . . in Asien und Europa und ihr Verhaeltnis zur slavischen Mythologie," Polska Akademia Umiejętności, Kraków. *Bulletin international*, 7-8 (1910) pp 97-115.

139. Demetrykiewicz, W. "O świeżo odkrytych śladach polichromji na posągu t.zw. Światowita," Polska Akademia Umiejetnosci, Kraków. *Sprawozdania z czynności i posiedzen*, 34 (1929) no. 6, p 18. (Concerning the recently discovered paint on the figure of the so called Swiatowit)

140. Derzhavin Nikolai Sevast'ianovich. "Perun v iazykovykh i fol'klornykh perezhivaniiakh u slavian," *Iazyk i literatura*, 3 (1929) pp 10-58. (Perun in the linguistic and folklore experiences of the Slavs)

141. Derzhavin, Nikolai Sevast'ianovich. "Perun v slavianskom fol'klore." in International Congress of Slavists. 1st., Prague, 1929. *Sbornik praci I. sjezdu slavanskych filologu v Praze 1929.* V Praze, Orbis, Sv.2 (1932) pp 45-8. French summary. (PG11.I5 1929) DLC ICU IU MiU NN (Perun in Slavic folklore)

142. Derzhavin, Nikolai Sevast'ianovich. "Religiia." in his *Slaviane v drevnosti; kulturno-istoricheskii ocherk*. Moskva, 1946. pp 134-61. (D147.D42) DLC CaBVaU CLSU CLU CSt CSt-H IaU ICRL ICU InU IU MH MiU NcD NcU NIC NN NNC OCU OrCS OU PU RPB TNJ ViU VtMiM *Great Britain*: BM *USSR*: LL (Religion)

143. Derzhavin, Nikolai Sevast'ianovich. "Troian" v "Slove o polku Igoreve," *Vestnik drevnei istorii*, 1939, no. 6, pp 159-77. (Troian in Slovo o polku Igoreve)

144. Derzhavin, Nikolai Sevast'ianovich. "Troian v Slove o polku Igoreve." in his *Sbornik statei i issledovanii v oblasti slavianskoi filologii*. Moskva–Leningrad, 1941. pp 5-60. (PG15.D4) DLC CaOTU CLSU CSt CtY ICU InU IU NcD NcU NN NNC OU PSt RPB TNJ TxU ViU WaU *USSR*: LL (Troian in Slovo o polku Igoreve)

145. Derzhavin, Nikolai Sevast'ianovich. "Troian" v "Slove o poklu Igoreve i v fol'klore iuzhnykh slavian." in his *Istoriia Bolgarii*. Moskva, 1945. t. 1, pp 206-11. (DR67.D4) DLC CaBVaU CLSU CSt CtY DS ICU InU MB MH MiU NN NNC OCl PSt ScU TxU ViU WaU *Great Britain*: BM *USSR*: LL (Troian in Slovo o polku Igoreve and in the folklore of the southern Slavs)

146. Dickenmann, E. "Serbokroatische Dabog," *Zeitschrift fuer slavische Philologie*, 20 (1950) pp 323-46.

147. Diels, Paul. Prove," *Archiv fuer slavische Philologie*, 40 (1925) p 156.

148. Dietz J. C. F. "Noch ein Versuch ueber Adams von Bremen und Helmolds Beschreibung von Rethra," *Neue Monatsschrift von und fuer Mecklenburg*, 1 (1792) pp 321-6.

149. Dintses, L. A. "Dokhristianskie khramy Rusi v svete pamiatnikov narodnogo iskusstva," *Sovetskaia etnografiia*, 1947, no. 2, pp 67-94. (The pre-Christian temples of Rus in light of the monuments of folk art)

150. Dittrich, Z. R. "Zur Religioesen Ur- und Fruehgeschichte der Slawen," *Jahrbuecher fuer Geschichte Osteuropas*, N.F. 9 (1961) pp 481-510.

151. Djordjadzé, Olga. "Sur une identification de Svarog-Sésostris," *Synthèses*, 168 (1960) pp 215-21.

152. Dobrowský, J. "Bemerkungen eines Boehmen ueber die Verwandtschaft der slawischen u. nordischen Mythologie," Prague. Národní museum. *Monatsschrift*, 1 (1827) pp 59-60.

153. Donnert, Erich. "Das Heidentum der Slawen in der schriftlichen Ueberlieferung der fraenkischen Fruezeit im 7 und 8, Jh.," *Slavica Gandensia*, 7-8 (1980-81) pp 31-40.

154. Dovgialo, G. I. "Dokhristianskie religioznye predstavleniia belorusov v svete obshcheindoevropeiskoi mifologii i sravnitel'nogo izucheniia religii (po povodu issledovanii Viach. Vs. Ivanova i V.N. Toporova)." in *Voprosy istorii drevnego mira i srednikh vekov.* F.M. Nechai, ed. Minsk, Izd. BGU, 1970. pp 164-78. (D53.V66) DLC CaOTU DDO ICU IEN InNd InU IU MB MH MU NcD NjP WU *USSR*: GPIB LL (The pre-Christian religious ideas of the Belorussians in the light of Indo-European mythology and the comparative study of religions (as regards the research of V.V. Ivanov and V.N. Toporov)

155. Dovzhenok, V. I. "Drevneslavianskie iazycheskie idoly iz sele Ivankovtsy v Podnestrov'e," Akademiia nauk SSSR. Institut arkheologii. *Kratkie soobshcheniia o dokladakh i polevykh issledovaniiakh*, 48 (1952) pp 136-41. (Ancient Slavic idols from the village of Ivankovtsa in the region of the lower Dnestr)

156. Dowiat, Jerzy. "Pogański obraz świata a przyczny chrystianizacji Słowian." in *Wieki średnie. Prace ofiarowane Tadeuszowi Manteufflowi w 60 rocznice urodzin.* Warszawa, Państwowe Wydawn. Naukowe, 1962. pp 79-86. (D119.W5) DLC CaBVaU CoU CtY CU ICU InU IU MH MiDW MiU NNC OU *Great Britain*: BM (The pagan view of the world and the causes for the Christianization of the Slavs)

157. Duichev, I. S. "K voprosu o iazycheskikh zhertvoprinosheniiakh v drevnei Rusi." in *Kul'turnoe nasledie Drevnei Rusi: istoki, stanovlenie, traditsii.* V. G. Bazanov, ed. Moskva, Nauka, 1976. pp 31-4. (PG3001.K78) DLC MChB MNS NBuU NIC VtMiM *USSR*: GPIB LL (Concerning pagan sacrifice in ancient Rus)

158. Duichev, I. S. "Le problème des tumuli et de sanctuaires slavs en Bulgarie," *Slavia antiqua*, 9 (1962) pp 61-70.

159. Dukova, U. "Zur Frage des iranischen Einflusses auf die slawische mythologische Lexik," *Zeitschrift fuer Slawistik*, 24 (1979) no. 1, pp 11-16.

160. Duridanov, I. "Urslaw. Perun und seine Spuren in der Toponymie," *Studia slavica*, 12 (1966) nos. 1-4, pp 99-102.

161. Dyggve, Ejnar. "Der Holztempel Svantevits und der Schuchhardtsche Baubefund zu Arkona." in International Congress of Prehistoric and Protohistoric Sciences, Hamburg, 1959. *Proceedings*, pp

250-1. (GN3.I54) DLC AzU CaBVaU CtY ICU InU KU NIC NN OU TxU WU

162. Dyggve, Ejnar. "Der slawische Viermastenbau auf Ruegen, beobachungen aus dem Swantewittempel des Saxo-Grammaticus," *Germania*, 37 (1959) pp 193-205.

163. Dziewulski, Władysław. *Postępy Chrystianizacji i proces likwidacji pogaństwa w Polsce wczesnofeudalnej.* Wrocław, Zakład Narodowy im. Ossolińskich, 1964. 206 p. (BR954.D9) DLC CLU ICU MB MH MiDW NcD NjPT NN ScU WaU *Great Britain*: BM (The advancement of Christianity and the liquidation of paganism in early Medieval Poland)

164. Eckermann, Karl. "Die Slawen (und Finnen)." in his *Lehrbuch der Religionsgeschichte und Mythologie der slavischen oder serbischen Staemme.* Halle, C.A. Schwetschke und suhn, 1848. v. 4, ab. 1-2, Exists in various editions. KU MeB MiU NN *France*: BN *USSR*: GPIB

165. Eckert, R. "Zu den Namen fuer weibliche mythologische Wesen auf -yn'i im slawischen," *Zeitschrift fuer Slawistik*, 22 (1977) no. 1, pp 44-52.

166. Eckhard, Tobias. *Discours von denen schwehr zu bekehrenden Wenden und daher eingefuehrten frembden deutschen Adel in dem Mecklenburgischen.* Quedlinburg, 1728. 20 p.

167. Eckhardus, M. P. J. *Duo monumenta agro Intreboncensi eruta, cum idolis Slavorum.* Wittembergae & Lipsiae, 1734. 334 p. *German Democratic Republic*: GLB

168. Efimenko, Petr Savvich. "O Iarile, iazycheskom bozhestve russkikh slavian," Geograficheskoe obshchestvo SSSR. *Zapiski po otdeleniiu etnografii*, 2 (1868) pp 79-112. (Concerning Jarilo, pagan god of the Russian Slavs) See no. 169

169. Efimenko, Petr Savvich. *O Iarile, iazycheskom bozhestve russkikh slavian.* St. Peterburg, 1869. 36 p. *USSR*: LL (Concerning Jarilo, pagan god of the Russian Slavs (See no. 168

170. Eichler, E. "Internationales Symposium ueber den slawischen Paganismus," *Zeitschrift fuer Slawistik*, 26 (1981) no. 2, pp 294-5.

171. Eisner, Jan. "Archeologické doklady o víře, kultu a magii dávného Slovana." in his *Rukovět Slovanské archeologie. Počátky Slovanů a jejich kultury*, Praha, Academia, 1966. pp 454-89. (GN549. S6E35) DLC CaBVaU CLU CSt CtY CU DDO ICU IEN InU IU LU MH MiU MnU MoU MU NcU NjP NN NNC NSyU

OrPS PPiU PSt RPB TxU ViU WaU *Great Britain*: BM (Archeological reports on the beliefs, cults, and magic of the early Slavs)

172. Ellis, Linda. "Reinterpretations of the West Slavic cult site in Arkona," *Journal of Indo-European Studies*, 6 (1978) nos. 1-2, pp 1-16.

173. Erben, Karl Jaromir. "Mitologia słowiański," *Niwa dwutygodnik*, 2 (1876) pp 342-52. (Slavic mythology)

174. Erben, Karl Jaromir. "O slavianskoi mifologii," *Russkaia besieda*, 2 (1857) no. 2, kn. 8, pp 71-128. (Concerning Slavic mythology)

175. Ettmueller, Ludwig. "Auch etwas ueber Flyns," *Neues Lausitzisches Magazin*, 22 (18440 pp 190-201.

176. Famintsyn, Aleksandr Sergeevich. *Bozhestva drevnikh slavian*. St. Petersburg, Tip. E. Arngol'da, 1884. 331 p. (BL930.F34) DLC CtY CU ICU MiU NIC NN NNC OCl RPB WU *USSR*: BAN GPIB LL Reviewed in Russia. Ministerstvo narodnogo prosveshcheniia. *Zhurnal*, 1885, ch. 239, otd. 2, pp 280-99. (The gods of the ancient Slavs)

177. Filipović, Milenko S. "Još o tragovima Perunova kuljta kod južnikh Slovena," Sarajevo. Zemaljski muzej. *Glasnik*, N.S. 9 (1954) pp 181-2. (Traces of Perun's cult among the southern Slavs)

178. Filipović, Milenko S. "Tragovi Perunova kuljta kod južnikh Slovena," Sarajevo, Zemaljski muzej. *Glasnik*, N.S. 3 (1948) pp 63-80. French and Russian summaries. (Traces of Perun's cult among the southern Slavs)

179. Filipović, Milenko S. "Zur Gottheit Mokoš bei den Suedslaven," *Die Welt der Slaven*, 6 (1961) no. 4, pp 393-400.

180. Filipowiak, Władysław. "Slavische Kultstaetten westpommerns im Lichte archaeologisch-toponomastischer Untersuchungen." in Congressus Internationalis Historiae Slavicae, Salisburog-Ratisbonensis, 2d, Universitaet Slazburg, 1967. *Das heidnische und christliche Slaventum*. Wiesbaden, O. Harrassowitz, 1969-70. v. 1, pp 75-80. (Series: Institutum Slavicum Salisburgo-Ratisbonese. Annales, Bd. II, 1) (PG11.C6 1967ae) DLC CaBVaU CaQMM CLU CoU CSt CU CU-SB CU-SC DeU FU GU ICU InU MB MiU MnU MoSCS MoSW NbU NBuU NcU NjP NjPT NN NNC NSyU OCU OKentU OrU OU PPT TxU WaU WU

181. Filipowiak, Władysław. "Słowiańskie miejsca kultowe Pomoraza Zachodniego w świetle badań archeologiczno-toponomastycznych," *Przegląd zachodnio-pomorskie*, 1 (1957) z. 5, pp 5-15. (The Slavic cult places of western Pomerania in light of archeological and toponymic research)

182. Filipowiak, Władysław. "Słowiańskie miejsca kultowe z Trzebiatowa," *Materiały zachodnio-pomorskie*, 3 (1957) pp 75-95. (Slavic cult places in Trzebiatow)

183. Filipowiak, Władysław & Wojtasik, J. "Światowit z Wolina," *Z otchłani wieków*, 41 (1975) no. 2, pp 82-8. (The Swiatowit from Wolin)

184. Fischer, Adam. "Kult Welesa u Słowian." in Narodopisná společnost československá, Prague. *Sborník prací věnovaných profesoru dru. Václav tillovi k šedesátým narozeninám 1867-1927.* Praha, Nakl. Orbis, 1927. pp 46-51. InU MH TxU *USSR*: LL (The Veles cult among the Slavs)

185. Fonvent, C de. *Mythologie greque, latine et slavonne, suivie d'un traite sur le chamonisme, le lamonisme et l'ancienne religion des differens peuples soumis a la Russie.* Moscou. Vsevolojsky, 1815. 176 p. DLC KU *France*: BN *USSR*: GPIB

186. Franck, B. O. "Goetzendienst und Orakel auf Arkona," *Griefswaldisches Academisches Archiv*, 1 (1817) H. 3, pp 91-111.

187. Franko, Ivan. "Wie man slavische Mythologie macht," *Archiv fuer slavische Philologie*, 29 (1907) pp 95-105.

188. Franz, Leonhard. *Falsche Slawengoetter. Eine iconographische Studie.* Leipzig, 1941, 46 p. (BL930.F7) DLC *Federal Republic of Germany*: JGH

189. Franz, Leonhard. *Falsche Slawengoetter. Eine iconographische Studie.* Bruenn, R. Rohrer, 1943. 81 p. CtY InU MH MH-AH NN OCl OU Reviewed in *Slavia occidentalis*, 18 (1947) p. 498.

190. Frenzel, Abraham. "Commentarius philologico-historicus de diis Soraborum aliorumque Slavorum." in Hoffmann, Christian Gottfried. *Scriptores rerum Lusaticarum antiqui & recentiores.* Lipsiae & Budissae, sumpt. D. Richteri, 1719. v. 2, pp 85-236. (DD491. L32S3) DLC *Great Britain*: BM

191. Frenzel, Michael. *Dissertationes historicae tres de idolis Slavorum.* Wittebergae, 1691-92. *Great Britain*: BM *USSR*: GPIB

192. Frenzel, Michael. "Dissertationes historicae tres de idolis Slavorum." in Hoffmann, Christian Gottfried. *Scriptores rerum Lusaticarum antique & recentiores.* Lipsiae & Budissae, sumpt. D. Richteri, 1719. v. 2, pp 63-84. (DD491.L32S3) DLC *Great Britain*: BM

193. Gajáry Kuhinka, Ernest M. *De toepassing van de phaenomenologische anthropologie op de godsdienst van de West-Slawen, Tsjechen,*

Slowaken, Lutsitsi-Sorben, Polen. Utrecht, 1952. 93 p. Summaries in English, German and French. (BL930.G3) DLC *Great Britain*: BM

194. Gal'kovskii, Nikolai Mikhailovich. *Bor'ba khristianstva s ostatkami iazychestva v drevnei Rusi.* Khar'kov, Eparkhial'naia tip., 1913-1916. 2v. Volume 2 entitled: *Drevne-russkie slova i poucheniia napravlennyia protiv ostatkov iazychestva v narode.* Exists in various editions. CoU ICU WU *USSR*: GPIB LL Reviewed in *Bogoslovskii viestnik*, 25 (1916) May, pp 190-99. (The struggle of Christianity with the remnants of paganism in ancient Rus)

195. Gasparini, Evel. *Credenze religiose e obblighi nuziali degli antichi Slavi.* Venice, La Goliardica, 1959. 283 p. MH *Great Britain*: BM *USSR*: ANSSSR-INION

196. Gasparini, Evel. "La cultura spirituale." in his *Il matriarcato slavo. Antropologia culturale dei proto-Slavi.* Firenze, Samsoni, 1973. pp 491-708. (GN549.S6G36) DLC CaBVaU CSt CtY MH MiU NIC NjP NN NNC *USSR*: ANSSSR-INION Reviewed in *History of Religions*, 14 (1974) no. 1, pp 74-8.

197. Gasparini, Evel. "Gli astri nella mitologia e nelle credenze populari dei Balto-Slavi," *Etnološki pregled*, 6-7 (1965) pp 21-37.

198. Gasparini, Evel. "Questioni di mitologia slava," *Slovenski etnograf*, 13 (1960) pp 91-113, 14 (1961) pp 91-114.

199. Gasparini, Evel. "Sul paganesimo degli antichi Slavi." Naples. Instituo orientale. Sezione slava. *Annali*, 8 (1965) pp 135-67.

200. Gąssowska, Eligia. "Sanktuarium pogańskie w Dobrzeszowie," *Z otchłani wieków*, 45 (1979) no. 2, pp 122-7. (The pagan sanctuary in Dobrzeszow)

201. Gąssowski, Jerzy. "Ośrodek kultówy na Łysej Gorze." in Gassowska, Eligia. *Łysa Gora we wczesnym średniowieczu.* Wrocław, 1970. pp 24-43. (Series: Instytut Historii Kultury Materialnej Polskiej Akademii Nauk. Polskie badania archeologiczne, t. 16) (GN845. P7G3) DLC CLU CSt CU DDO IU MiDW MiU NcD NIC NNC OU (The cult center on Lysa Gora)

202. Gąssowski, Jerzy. "Ośrodek kultu pogańskiego na Łysej Górze." in *Religia pogańskich Słowian; sesja naukowa w Kielcach.* Kielce, 1968. pp 47-60. (The pagan cult center on Lysa Gora) See no. 635

203. Gąssowski, Jerzy. "Religia pogańskich Słowian i jej przezytki we wczesnym Chrześcijanstwie," *Archeologia Polski*, 16 (1971) no.

1-2, pp 557-74. French summary. (The religion of the pagan
Slavs and its remnants in early Christianity)

204. Gąssowski, Jerzy. "Les religions païennes des slaves occidentaux a la
lumière des recherches archeologiques et les survivances du
paganisme dans le haut Moyen age." in *Congres International
d'Archeologie Slave*, 1st, Warsaw, 1965. Wrocław, Zakład Narodowy im. Ossolińskich, v. 5, pp 388-93. (GN700.C58 1965) DLC
CaBVaU CaOTP CaQMM CLU CoU CSt CtY CU DDO DSI
FU IaU ICU InNd InU IU MH MH-P MiU MnU MoU MU
NcD NcU NjP NN NNC OU TxU

205. Gąssowski, Jerzy. "Ślady ośrodka kultowego na Łysej Górze," *Acta
archeologica Carpathica*, 1 (1959) z. 2, pp 297-99. French summary. (The remains of a cult center on Lysa gora)

206. Gaster, M. "Rumaenische Beitraege zur russischen Goetterlehre,"
Archiv fuer slavische Philologie, 28 (1906) pp 575-83.

207. Gediga, Bogusław. *Śladami religii prasłowian*. Wrocław, Ossolineum,
1976. 285 p. (BL930.G4) DLC CU IU MH MiDW NcU NIC
NjP NN OClW WaU WU *USSR*: BANLit BBeloSSR BLitSSR
GBIL GPIB KharGU LL LvovGB OdessaGB VilGU (On the
trial of the pre-Slavic religion)

208. Georgiev, Iordan. *Staritě i dnešnitě vervanija na Bulgaritě*. Tirnova,
1900. 32 p. (Past and present belief in Bulgaria)

209. Georgiev, Vladimir I. "Indoevropeiskii termin *Deywos v slavian-
skikh iazykakh." in *To honor Roman Jakobson. Essays on the
occasion of his seventieth birthday, 11 October 1966*. The Hague,
Paris, Mouton, 1967. v. 1, pp 734-7. (Series: Janua linguarum,
series maior, v. 31-33) (P26.J32) DLC AU CaBVaU CLSU
CnOS CoFS CoU CSt CtW CU-S DAU DDO DSI FTaSU FU
GAT GU IaAS IaU IEdS InU IU KU KyU LU MdBJ MdU
MeB MH MiEM MnS MnU MoSW MoU MWelC NBC NbU
NjR NRU NSyU OClW OkS PPiU PPULC ScU TU TxHR UU
ViU VtU *France*: BN *USSR*: ANSSSR-INION BAN BANUkr
GBIL LL SS (The Indoeuropean term *Deywos in the Slavic
languages)

210. Georgiev, Vladimir I. "Slawischer Wortschatz und Mythologie,"
Anzeiger fuer slavische Philologie, 6 (1972) pp 20-6.

211. Georgiev, Vladimir I. "Trite fazi na slavianskata mitologiia." in
Izsledvaniia v chest na Akademik Mikhail Arnaudov. Sofia, BAN,
1970. pp 469-75. (PG1003.I9) DLC AAP CaOTU CSt CtY CU
CU-SB ICU InU IU MH MiEM MiU NjP NNC PPiU PSt RPB
TxU ViU WaU (Three phases of Slavic mythology)

212. Gerasimov, Todor. "Svedenie za edin mramoren idol u bulgarskite slaviani v Solnsko." in Bulgarska Akademiia na Naukite, Sofia. Otdelenie za Ezikoznanie, Literaturoznanie i Etnografiia. *Ezikovedsko-etnografski izsledvaniia v pamet na Akademik Stoian Romanski.* Sofia, BAN 1960. pp 557-61. (PG807.B85) DLC CaOTU CLU CoU CSt CU ICU InU IU MdU MiU MnU NcD NjP NN NNC NSyU OU RPB TxU ViU WU *Great Britain*: BM *USSR*: GPIB LL (Information about a marble idol among the Bulgarian Slavs in Solnsko)

213. Gergowicz, Edmund S. *Mitologia słowiański w zarysie.* Lvov, 1872. 59 p. *Great Britain*: BM Reviewed in *Biblioteka warszawska,* 1872, no. 3, pp 461-5. (An outline of Slavic mythology)

214. Gierlach, Boguslaw. *Sanktuaria słowiańskie.* Warszawa, Iskry, 1980. 234 p. (BL930.G55) DLC InU KU MH MiDW OU ViU WU (Slavic sanctuaries)

215. Giesebrecht, H. L. T. "Religion und Cultus der Wenden." in his *Wendische Geschichte aus Jahren 780 bis 1182.* Berlin, R. Gaertner, 1843. v. 1, pp 57-94. CU MB MdBJ MH MiU TxDaM-P *Great Britain*: BM *France*: BN

216. Giesebrecht, H. L. T. "Von der Religion der wendischen Voelker an der Ostsee," *Baltische Studien,* 6 (1839) H. 1, pp 128-61.

217. Gieysztor, Aleksander. *Mitologia Słowian.* Warszawa, Wydawnictwa Artystyczne i Filmowe, 1982. 272 p. CU MU OU PPiU (Slavic mythology)

218. Gieysztor, Aleksander. "Mythologie slave." in Grimal, P. ed. *Mythologies des montages, des forêts et des îles.* Paris, Larousse, 1963. pp 82-97. (BL311.G7) DLC CU IU MH NIC NN

219. Gieysztor, Aleksander. "La mythologie slave, le modèle trifonctionnel et la culture populaire." in International Congress of Historical Sciences, 15th, Bucharest. *La Pologne au XVe Congrès International des Sciences Historique à Bucarest.* Wroclaw, Ossolineum, 1980. pp 11-24. AzU InU KU MiEM NBuU NcD NcU ViU

220. Gieysztor Aleksander. "The Slavic pantheon and new comparative mythology," *Quaestiones Medii Aevi,* 1 (1977) pp 7-32.

221. Gieysztor, Aleksander. "The Slavic pantheon and the new comparative mythology," Harvard. University. Seminar on Ukrainian Studies. *Minutes,* 5 (1974-75) pp 82-84.

222. Gieysztor, Aleksander. "Sprawca piorunów w mitologii słowiańskiej." in *Ars historica: prace z dziejow powszechnych i Polski.* Marian Biskup, ed. Poznan, Uniwersytet im. Adama Mickiewicza, 1976.

pp 155-61. (DK4150.A77) DLC InNd InU KU MiDW MiU NoU NIC NjP PU UU (The lightning giver in Slavic mythology)

223. Gimbutas, Marija. "Ancient Slavic religion: a synopsis." in *To honor Roman Jakobson. Essays on the occasion of his seventieth birthday, 11 October 1966.* The Hague, Paris Mouton, 1967. v. 1, pp 738-59. (Series: Janua linguarum, series maior, v. 31-33) (P26.J32) For locations, see no. 209

224. Gimbutas, Marija. "Perkunas/Perun, the thunder god of the Balts and the Slavs," *Journal of Indo-European studies,* 1 (1973) pp 466-78.

225. Gimbutas, Marija. "Religion." in her *The Slavs.* New York, Praeger, 1971. pp 151-70. (Series: Ancient peoples and places, v. 74) (D147.G54) DLC CSt CtY GU InU KU MB MH MiU MoSW NBuU NcU NjP OkU OrU OU PSt RPB TxU ViU WaU

226. Glagolev, A. "Mifologiia," *Vestnik Evropy,* 1815, ch. 80, no. 5-6, pp 97-108. (Mythology)

227. Glinka, Grigorii Andreevich. *Drevniaia religiia slavian.* Mitava, V tip. I.F. Shtefengagena i syna, 1804. 150 p. (BL930.G6) DLC *Great Britain*: BM *USSR*: BAN GPIB (The ancient religion of the Slavs)

228. Glinka, Grigorii Andreevich. "Khram Svietovida," *Vestnik Evropy,* 1803, ch. 10, no. 15, pp 173-86. (The temple of Swiatowit)

229. Glueckselig, Anton Thormond. (G.T. Legis pseud.) *Alkuna. Nordische und nordslawische Mythologie.* Leipzig C.H.F. Hartmann, 1831. 239 p. IEN IU MBAt MH NIC NN OCl RPB *USSR*: GPIB

230. Goetz, G. "Die Prillwitzer Idole," Deutsche Gesellschaft fuer Anthropologie, Ethnologie und Urgeschichte. *Korrespondenz-Blatt,* 12 (1881) p 39.

231. Golovatskii, Iakov Fedorovich. *Ocherk staroslavianskogo basnosloviia.* Lvov, Tip. Stavropigiiskogo Instituta, 1860. 108 p. NNC OCl *USSR*: GPIB LL Reviewed in Prague. Narodni Museum. *Časopis,* 38 (1864) pp 218-21. (Ann essay on old Slavic folklore)

232. Gorodtsov, V. A. "Dako-sarmatskie elementy v russkom religioznym tvorchestve," Moscow. Gosudarstvenny istoricheskii muzei. *Trudy,* 1 (1926) pp 6-35. (The Dacian-Sarmatian elements in Russian religious work)

233. "Die Gottheiten der heidnischen Sorben im Meissnerlande," *Das Vaterland der Sachsen,* 3 (1845) lief 26, pp 115-6.

234. Gringmuth-Dallmer, Elke & Hollnagel, Adolf. "Dwogłowe bóstwo słowian," *Z otchłani wieków*, 37 (1971) no. 4, pp 271-4. (The two-headed god of the Slavs)

235. Grudziński, T. "Pogaństwo i Chrześcijanstwo w świadomości społecznej Polski wczesnofeudalnej." in Powszechny zjazd historyków Polskich. 9th, Warsaw, 1963. *Historia kultury średniowiecznej w Polsce.* Aleksander Gieysztor, ed. Wraszawa, Polskie tow. historyczne, 1963. pp 33-59. CSt-H MH MiU NcD (Paganism and Christianity in the consciousness of early feudal Polish society)

236. Gržetić, Nikola. *O vjeri starih slovjena.* Mostar, Tiskano pisčevom nakladom u Hrvatskoj Dion. Tiskarni, 1900– (BL930.G7) DLC ICU NNC TxU Reviewed in *Nastavni vjesnik*, 9 (1901) pp 475-83. (Concerning the beliefs of the old Slavs)

237. Grzymkowski, Andrzej. "Kamienne bóstwo pogańskie z Małocina," *Z otchłani wieków*, 1976, no. 3, pp 247-53. (Pagan stone gods from Malocin)

238. Gurevich, F. D. "Kamennye idoly sebezhskogo muzeia," Akademiia nauk SSSR. Institut arkheologii. *Kratkie soobshcheniia o dokladakh i polevykh issledovaniiakh*, 54 (1954) pp 176-9. (The stone idols of the Sebezhskii museum)

239. Gurevich F. D. "Zbruchskii idol." in *Etnogenez vostochnykh slavian.* Moskva–Leningrad, 1941. pp 279-87. French summary. (Series: Materialy i issledovaniia po arkheologii SSSR, no. 6) (DK30.M4 no. 6) DLC IU *USSR*: GPIB LL (The Zbruch idol)

240. Guseva, N. R. "K voprosu o znachenii imen nekotorykh personazhei slavianskogo iazychestva." in *Lichnye imena v proshlom, nastoiashchem, budushchem. Problemy antroponimiki.* Moskva, Nauka, 1970. V.A. Nikonov, ed. pp 334-9. (CS2375.R9L5) DLC CaOTU CaQMM CtY CU CU-SB GU IaAS ICU InU IU MB MCM MdU MH MiDW MiEM MiU MnU MoSW MU BNC NcD NcU NIC NjP NN NNC NRU NSyU OrU PPiU PPT PSt RPB TNJ TU TxU ViU VtMiM WU *USSR*: LL (Concerning the meaning of the names of some of the personages of Slavic paganism)

241. Haas, Alfred. *Arkona in Jahre 1168.* Stettin, 1925. 62 p. *Federal Repubilc of Germany*: JGH

242. Haas, Alfred. "Slawische Kultstaetten auf der Inseln Ruegen," *Pommersche Jahrbuecher*, 19 (1918) pp 1-76.

244. Hadaczek, K. "Światowit," Polska Akademia Umiejętności, Krakow. Komisja antropologiczna. *Materyały antropologiczno-archeologiczne i etnograficzne*, 7 (1904) pp 114-21. (Swiatowit)

245. Hagenow, Friedrich von. *Beschreibung der auf der grossherzoglichen bibliothek zu Neustrelitz befindlichen Runensteine, und Versuch zur Erklaerung der auf denselben befindlichen Inschriften, nebst einigen neuen Nachrichten ueber die Fundoeter derselben und der dort ebenfalls befindlichen slavischen Gottheiten.* Loitz, bei dem verfasser Greiswald, 1826. 25 p. CtY MH NIC *Great Britain*: BM

246. Hammerstein, W. "Echte wendische Goetzen," *Mecklenburgische Jahrbuecher*, 37 (1872) pp 172-9, 38 (1873) pp 238-9.

247. Hammerstein, W. "Ueber den wendischen Gott Zuarzici," *Mecklenburgische Jahrbuecher*, 37 (1872) pp 180-2.

248. Hane, P. H. "Conjectur ueber eine Stelle des Helmolds das Pantheon zu Rhetra betreffend," *Neue Monatsschrift von und fuer Mecklenburg*, 2 (1789) pp 735-54, 827-44, 1031-44.

249. Hanika, Joseph. "Zur Problematik des alttscheschischen Zelu," *Die Welt der Slaven*, 2 (1957) no. 3, pp 314-21.

250. Hanuš, Ignác Jan. *Bájeslovný kalendář slovanský, čili požustatky pohansko-svátečných obřaduv slovanských.* V Praze, Kober & Markgraf, 1860. 264 p. (BL935.S6H3) DLC MH *Great Britain*: BM (Slavic folklore calendar, that is the remaining Slavic pagan rites)

251. Hanuš, Ignác Jan. *Děva, zlatovlasá bohyně poganských Slovanův.* Praha, Tisk Kateřiny Jeřábkove, 1860. 40 p. MH *USSR*: GPIB LL (Deva, the goldenhaired goddess of the pagan Slavs) See no. 252

252. Hanuš, Ignác Jan. "Děva, zlatovlasá bohyně pohanských Slovanů," Česká společnost nauk, Prgue. *Abhandlungen*, Folge 5, v. 11 (1861) pp 259-98. (Deva, the goldenhaired goddess of the pagan Slavs) See no. 251

253. Hanuš, Ignác Jan. "O bohyni Živě," Prague, národní museum. *Časopis*, 6 (1865) pp 123-39. (Concerning the goddess Živa)

254. Hanuš, Ignác Jan. "Ueber das Wesen und Ursprung der slawischen Mythologie," Akademie der Wissenschaften, Berlin. *Sitzungsberichte*, 1865, July–December, pp 22-36.

255. Hanuš, Ignác Jan. *Die Wissenschaft des slawischen Mythus.* Lvov, J. Millikowski, 1842. 432 p. ICN ICU InU MdBP MH MiU NN

OCl PBm PU *USSR:* GPIB LL Reviewed in *Jahrbuecher fuer slawische Literatur, Kunst, und Wissenshcaft,* 1 (1843) no. 1, pp 64-8.

256. Harisch, "Sorbenwendische goetzen," *Neues Lausitzisches Magazin,* 6 (1827) pp 301-24.

257. Haškovec, Miroslav. "Jeste Triglav-Teruvan." in *Slovanský sborník, věnovaný jeho magneficenci prof. Františku Pastrnkovi rektoru University Karlovy k sedemdesátym narozeninám 1853-1923.* V Praze, Vydal Klub modernich filologů, 1923. pp 58-65. (PG14.P3) DLC CoU CSt DDO ICU IU MH MiU NjP (Triglav-Teruvan)

258. Haupt, Gerog. "Der Kopf von Jankowo," *Aus dem Posener Lande,* 4 (1909) August, pp 313-4.

259. Heckowa, Kazimierz Wand. *Podznakiem świętego słońca; dawne wierzenia śląskie.* Wrocław, Zakład Narodowy im. Ossolińskich, 1961. 125 p. (BL930.H4) DLC ICU MH OU *Great Britain:* BM *USSR:* OdessaGU (Concerning the holy sun; early Silesian beliefs)

260. "Heidnische gottheiten der Weiss-Russen," *Archiv fuer wissenschaftliche Kunde von Russland,* 5 (1847) pp 626-39.

261. Hensel, Witold. "Wczesnosredniowieczna figurka czterotwarzowego bostwa z Wolina," *Slovenska archeologia,* 26 (1978) no. 1, pp 13-7. French summary. (The early medieval figure of a four faced god from Wolin)

262. Hering, "Flins," *Lasizische Monatsschrift,* 1796, no. 2, p 19.

263. Herrmann, Joachim. "Arkona auf Ruegen. Tempelburg und politisches Zentrum der Ranen vom 9. bis 12. Jh. Ergebnisse der archaeologischen Ausgrabungen 1969-71," *Zeitschrift fuer Archaeologie,* 8 (1974) no. 2, pp 177-209.

264. Herrmann, Joachim. "Edifices et objets sculptes à destination culturelle chez les tribus slaves du nord-ouest entre le VIIe et le XIIe siècles," *Slavica Gandensia,* 7-8 (1980-81) pp 41-68.

265. Herrmann, Joachim. "Einige Bemerkungen zu Tempelstaetten und Kultbildern im nordwestslawischen Gebiet," *Archeologia Polski,* 16 (1971) nos. 1-2, pp 525-40.

266. Herrmann, Joachim. "Geistige und kultisch-religioese Vorstellung der Nordwestslaven und ihre Widerspiegelung in den archaeologischen Quellen." in Congressus Internationalis Historiae Slavicae, Salisburgo-Ratisbonensis, 2d, Universitaet Salzburg, 1967. *Das*

heidnische und christliche Slaventum. Wiesbaden, O. Harrasso-witz, 1969-70. v. 1, pp 60-74. (Series: Institutum Slavicum Salisburgo-Ratisbonese. Annales, Bd. II, 1) (PG11.C6 1967ae) For locations, see no. 180.

267. Herrmann, Joachim. "Religion und Kult." in *Die Slawen in Deutschland. Geschichte u. Kultur d. slaw. Staemme westl. v Oder v Neisse vom 6.-12. Jh.* Berlin, Akademie-Verl., 1970. pp 249-62. (DD734.S5) DLC CaQMM CLU CoU CSt CtY CU CU-S CU-SC GU IaAS IaU ICU IEN InU IU KyU MB MdU MH MiDW MiEM MiU MnU MoSW MU NjP NjR NNC NSyU OU PPiU PSt ViU VtU WU

268. Herrmann, Joachim. "Zu den kulturgeschichtlichen Wurzeln und zur historischen Rolle nordwestslawischer Tempel des fruehen Mittelalters," *Slovenska archeologia,* 26 (1978) no. 1, pp 19-28.

269. Hodál, Juraj. *O pohanskom náboženstve starých slovákov.* Trnava. Nákl. Spolku Sv. Vojtecha, 1925. 24 p. IU (Concerning the pagan worship of the old Slovaks)

270. Hoenig, Anton. *Die slawische Mythologie in der tschechischen und slowakischen Literatur.* Augsburg, Blasaditsch, 1976. 210 p. (PG5003.2M9H6) DLC InU MnU PU

271. Holsten, Robert. "Aus der Religionsgeschichte der pommerschen Slaven," *Zeitschrift fuer slavische Philologie,* 19 (1947) pp 1-6.

272. Hopkins, Edward Washburn. "Religion of the Slavic peoples." in his *History of Religions.* New York, 1918, pp 138-48. Exists in various editions. (BL80.H6) DLC CU LU MB MiU NIC NN OCl OU PU ViU

273. Horoško, Leŭ. "A guide to Byelorussian mythology," *Journal of Byelorussian Studies,* 1 (1966) no. 2, pp 68-79.

274. Iavin, V. L. "Sviatilishche Peruna." in *Po sledam drevnikh kul'tur.* Moskva, Gos. Izd-vo Kul'turno-prosvetitel'noi Lit-ry, 1953. pp 250-1. (DK30.P57) DLC CaBVaU CaOTU CLU CSt CtY CU DDO ICU InU IU MH-P NBC NcD NIC NjP NN NNC OrCS OrU OU RPB TxU WaU *USSR:* GPIB LL (Perun's sanctuary)

275. "Iazycheskie verovaniia v drevnei Rostovskoi oblasti," *Iaroslavskie eparkhial'nye vedomosti,* 1868, no. 4, pp 27-31. (Pagan beliefs in the ancient Rostov regon)

276. Ilarion, Metropolitan of Winnipeg and all Canada. *Dokhrystyians'ki viruvannia ukrains'koho narodu.* Winnipeg, Volyn, 1965. 424 p.

(BL980.R8I4) DLC CaOTU CLU CU InU IU KU MH MiU NBuU NjP NSyU OCU TNJ-R WU (The pre-Christian beliefs of the Ukrainian people)

277. Il'inskii. G. A. "Do kritiki kanonu volodimirovikh bogiv," Akademiia nauk URSR, Kiev. Istorychna sektsiia. *Zapysky*. 20 (1925) pp 11-5. (A criticism of the list of Vladimr's gods)

278. Il'inskii. G. A. "Iz istorii drevne-slavianskikh iazycheskikh verovanii," Kazan. Universitet. Obshchestvo arkheologii, istorii i etnografii. *Izvestiia*, 29 (1922) no. 3-4, pp 5-9. (From the history of ancient Slavic pagan beliefs)

279. Il'inskii. G. A. "Odno neizvestnoe drevneslavianskoe bozhestvo," Akademiia nauk SSSR. *Izvestiia VI seriia*, 21 (1927) no. 5-6, pp 369-72. (An unknown ancient Slavic God)

280. Il'inskii. G. A. "Podaga." in *Mélanges de philologie offerts à m. J.J. Mikkola . . . à l'occasion de son soixante-cinquième anniversaire le 6 juillet 1931 par ses amis et ses élèvs*. Helsinki, Druckerei A.G. der finnischen Literaturgesellschaft, 1931. pp 45-6. (Series: Suomalainen tiedeakajemia, Helsinki. Toiituksia, ser B, t. 27) DDO ICU InU NNC OCl RPB *Great Britain*: BM

281. Il'inskii. G. A. "Pripegala," *Prace filologiczne*, 12 (1927) pp 416-20.

282. Ingemann, Bernhard Severin. *Grundtraek til en nord-slavisk og vendish gudeloere*. Kjobenhavn, Trysk his J.H. Schultz, 1824. 38 p. ICN

283. Ionescu, A. I. "Les plus archaïques representations des êtres surnaturels dans le croyances populaires des slaves," *Bulgarian Historical Review*, 4 (1976) no. 3, pp 38-51.

284. "Ist die Echtheit der obotritischen Alterthuemer in Neustrelitz gegen jeden Zweifel sicher gestellt," *Freimuethiges Abenblatt*, 9 (1827) no 464, pp 956-8.

285. "Istoricheskoe obozrenie mifologii severnykh narodov Evropy," *Moskovskii telegraf*, 1827, ch. 14, no. 7, pp 167-90, no. 8, pp 251-78, ch. 15, no. 9, pp 25-34. (A historical review of the mythology of the northern peoples of Europe)

286. Ivakin, G. IU. "Sviashchennyi dub iazycheskikh slavian," *Sovetskaia etnografiia*, 1979, no. 2, pp 106-115. (The sacred oak of the pagan Slavs)

287. Ivakin, G. IU. "Sviashchennyi dub Peruna." in *Drevnosti srednego Podneprov'ia. Sbornik nauchnykh trudov*. Kiev, Naukova Dumka, 1981. pp 124-36. *USSR*: GPIB LL (The sacred oak of Perun)

288. Ivakin, G. IU. & Gupalo, K. N. "Sviashchennyi dub slavian." in Akademiia nauk SSSR. Institut arkheologii. *Arkheologicheskie otkrytiia 1976 goda.* Moskva, Nauka, 1977. pp 300-1. (The sacred oak of the Slavs)

289. Ivanov, Iordan. "Kul't Perun u iuzhnikh slaviane," Akademiia nauk SSSR. Otdelenie russkogo iazyka i slovesnosti. *Izvestiia*, 8 (1902) kn. 4, pp 140-74. (The Perun cult among the southern Slavs)

290. Ivanov, Viacheslav Vsevolodovich & Toporov, Vladimir Nikolaevich. *Issledovaniia v oblasti slavianskikh drevnostei.* Moskva, Nauka, 1974. 340 p. (BL930.I93) DLC AkU CaBVaU CaOTU CaQMM CU CU-SB DGW InU IU KU MB MdU MH MiEM MnU MoSW MoU MU NcD NcU NFQC NhD NIC NjP NN NRU NSyU OrU PPiU TNJ ViBlbV ViU VtMiM *USSR*: GPIB LL Reviewed in *Slavia antiqua*, 24 (1977) pp 305-16. (Research in the field of Slavic antiquities)

291. Ivanov, Viacheslav Vsevolodovich. "K etimologii baltiiskogo i slavianskogo nazvanii boga groma," *Voprosy slavianskogo iazykoznaniia*, 1958, vyp. 3, pp 101-11. (Concerning the etymology of the Baltic and Slavic name of the god of thunder)

292. Ivanov, Viacheslav Vsevolodovich & Toporov, Vladimir Nikolaevich. "K probleme dostovernosti pozdnikh vtorichnykh istochnikov v sviazi s issledovaniiami v oblasti mifologii (Dannye o Velese v traditsiiakh severnoi Rusi i voprosy kritiki pis'mennykh tekstov," Tartu. Ülikool. *Trudy po znakovym sistemam*, 1973, no. 6, pp 46-82. (On the problem of the reliability of late secondary sources in connection with studies in mythology (Data on Veles in the tradition of northern Rus' and questions of the criticism of written texts)

293. Ivanov, Viacheslav Vsevolodovich & Toporov, Vladimir Nikolaevich. "K semioticheskomu analizu mifa i rituala (na belorusskom materiale)." in *Sign. Language. Culture.* The Hague, Mouton, 1970. pp 325-89. (P325.S54) (Series: Janua linguarum. series maior, 1) DLC CaBVaU CaOTP CLSU CoU CSt CtY CU FU IaU ICU InU KyU MdBJ MH MiEM MoSW NcD NcU NIC NjP NN NRU OrU OU PSt TxU ViU VtU WU (Toward a semiotic analysis of myth and ritual (based on Belorussian material)

294. Ivanov, Viacheslav Vsevolodovich & Toporov, Vladimir Nikolaevich. "Mifologicheskie geograficheskie nazvaniia kak istochnik dlia rekonstruktsii etnogeneza i drevneishei istorii slavian." in *Vopro-*

sy etnogeneza i etnicheskoi istorii slavian i vostochnykh romantsev. Metodologiia i istoriografiia. V.D. Koroliuk, ed. Moskva, Nauka, 1976. pp 109-28. (D147.V64) DLC IU NIC NN *USSR:* GPIB LL (Mythological geographical names as a source for the reconstruction of the ethnogeneis and the ancient history of the Slavs)

295. Ivanov, Viacheslav Vsevolodovich & Toporov, Vladimir Nikolaevich. "Ob otrazhenii v belorusskom (iazyke) gruppy indoevropeiskikh slov, sviazannykh s kul'tom boga groma." in *Beloruskaia leksikalohiia i etymalohia. Prahrama i tezisy dakladau mizhrespublikanskai kanferentsyi.* Minsk, 1968. pp 58-9. *USSR:* LL (Concerning the reflections in Belorussian of a group of Indoeuropean words, connected with the cult of the thunder god)

296. Ivanov, Viacheslav Vsevolodovich. *Slavianskie iazykovye modeliruiushchie semioticheskie sistemy: drevnii period.* Moskva, Nauka, 1965. 245 p. (PG310.I9) DLC CaBVaU CaOTU CLU CoU CtY CU CU-SB IaU ICU IEN IU KU MH MiDW MiEM MiU MnU MoU MU NBC NcD NhD NjP NN NNC NRU NSyU OClW OrU OU PPiU PSt RPB TNJ TxU ViU WaU WU *Great Britain:* BM *France:* BN *USSR:* LL (Slavic semiotic linguistic modeling systems: the ancient period)

297. Ivanov, Viacheslav Vsevolodovich & Toporov, Vladimir Nikolaevich. "Vklad R.O. Iakobsona v slavianskie i indoevropeiskie fol'klornye mifologicheskie issledovaniia." in *Roman Jakobson: echoes of his scholarship.* Daniel Armstrong & C.H. Van Schooneveld, eds. Lisse, Peter de Ridder Press, 1977. pp 163-84. (P26.J3R6) DLC AzU CLSU CoU CtY FU GU IaAS KyU LU MdBJ MiDW MoSW NcU NjP NRU PPiU PU TNJ TxHR WU (The contribution of R.O. Jakobson to Slavic and Indoeuropean folklore and mythological research)

298. Jagič, Vatroslav. "Mythologische Skizzen. I. Svarog-Svarozic. II. Dazbog-Dabog," *Archiv fuer slavische Philologie,* 4 (1880) pp 412-27, 5 (1881) pp 1-14.

299. Jagič, Vatroslav. "Ein Nachtrag zur Frage ueber Dabog," *Archiv fuer slavische Philologie,* 5 (1881) pp 16-7.

300. Jagič, Vatroslav. "Eine Notiz zur slavische Mythologie," *Archiv fuer slavische Philologie,* 9 (1886) p 529.

301. Jagič, Vatroslav. "Zum Dazdbog," *Archiv fuer slavische Philologie,* 8 (1885) p 665.

302. Jagič, Vatroslav. "Zur slavischen Mythologie," *Archiv fuer slavische Philologie,* 37 (1920) pp 492-511.

303. Jakobson, Roman. "The Slavic God Veles and his Indo-European cognates." in *Studi linguistici in onore Vittore Pisani.* Torino, Paideia, 1969. pp 579-99. (P26.P5) DLC CaBVaU CLU CsT CU ICU IU MiDW MoU NIC NjP OCU OrU *France*: BN *USSR*: ANSSSR-INION BAN GBIL

304. Jakboson, Roman. "Voprosy sravnitel'noi indoevropeiskoi mifologii v svete slavianskikh pokazanii." in International Congress of Slavists, 6th, Prague, 1968. *American contributions to the sixth International Congress of Slavists. Prague, 1968, Aug 7-13.* The Hague, Mouton, 1968. v. 1, pp 125-8. (Series: Slavistic printings and reprintings, 80-1) (PG11.I5 1968c) DLC CaBVaU CaOTU CaQMM CLSU CoU CSt CtY CU FU GU IaAS IaU ICU InU IU KU KyU LU MB MdBJ MH MiU MnU MoSW MoU NbU NBuU NcD NcU NIC NNC NSyU OO OrU PPiU PSt RPB TNJ TU TxU ViU WaU WU (Questions of comparative Indo-european mythology in light of Slavic evidence)

305. Jakubowski, Stanisław. *Bogowie słowian. (Mitologja słowiańska).* Przemysl, Wydawno nakładem spółki wydawniczej "Praca i Książka", 1920. 16 p. MH *Great Britain*: BM (Gods of the Slavs) (Slavic mythology)

306. Jakubowski, Stanisław. *Bogowie słowian. The Gods of the Slavs.* Krakow, 1933. 58 p. Text in Polish, English, and French. CtY ICU InU NN (Gods of the Slavs)

307. Janosz, Stanislaw. "Wczesnośredniowieczne miejsce kultowe w północnozachodniej Wielkopolsce," *Fontes archaeologici Posnaniense,* 20 (1969) pp 218-30. French and German summaries. (Early medieval cult places in northwest Poland)

308. Jenč, K. A. "K prašenju wo póhanskich kultnych městnach Hornjeje Łužicy," Maćica Serbska, Bautzen. *Časopis,* 1910, pp 48-68, 81-126, 1911, pp 3-21. (Concerning the pagan cult places of Upper Lusatia)

309. Jenč, K. A. "Přibóh Flinc," Maćica Serbska, Bautzen. *Časopis,* 22 (1869) pp 9-41. (The god Flins)

310. Jenč, K. A. "Přibóh Swjantowit a jeho rozłamanje w lěće 1168," *Lužičan,* 1860, no. 3, pp 37-44, no. 4, pp 51-4. (The god Swiatowit and his destruction in 1168)

311. Jenč, K. A. "Přibóh Triglav," *Lužičan,* 1864, no. 2, pp 26-8. (The god Triglav)

312. Jenč, K. A. "Rhetra a Radegast," *Lužičan,* 1864, no. 1, pp 13-5. (Rethra and Radegast)

313. Jireček J. "O slovanském bohu Veselu," Prague. Národní museum. *Časopis*, 49 (1875) pp 405-16. (Concerning the Slavic god Veles)

314. Jireček, J. "Studia z oboru mythologie české," Prague. Národní museum. *Časopis*, 37 (1863) pp 1-28, 141-66, 262-69. (A study in the field of Czech mythology)

315. Johnson, Charles. "The Gods of the Slavs and Scythians," *Academy and Literature*, 3 (1891) no. 7, p 114.

316. Jungmann, A. "Krátký obsah náboženství pohanského u Slovanů," *Krok*, 2 (1828) no. 3, pp 339-92. (A brief discussion of the pagan religion of the Slavs)

317. K., M. *O religii pogańskickh Słowian*. Lvov, Seyfarta & Czajkowski, 1894. 67 p. *Great Britain*: BM Reviewed in *Kwartalnik historyczny*, 1895, p 677. (Concerning the religion of the pagan Slavs)

318. Kačarov, Gavril. "Po slavianskata mitologiia," Bŭlgarsko knizhovno druzhestvo. *Periodichesko spisanie*, 18 (1906) kn. 67, pp 811-2. (Concerning Slavic mythology)

319. Kačarov, Gavril. "Prinos kum religiiata na mnogoglavite bozhestva," Bulgarska akademiia na naukite, Sofia. Arkheologicheski Institut. *Izvestiia*, 17 (1950) pp 1-10. (A contribution to religion concerning multiheaded gods)

320. Kagarov, Evgenii Georgievich. *Religiia drevnikh slavian*. Moskva, Praktich. Znaniia, 1918. 73 p. CSt-H IU *USSR*: GPIB LL (The religion of the ancient Slavs)

321. Kaisarov, Andrei Sergeevich. "Opyt slovenskoi mifologii," *Moskovskiia uchenyia viedomosti*, 1805, no. 6, pp 41-44. (The test of Slavic mythology)

322. Kaisarov, Andrei Sergeevich. *Slavianskaia i rossiskaia mifologiia*. Moskva, V tip. Dubrovina i Merzliakova, 1807. 211 p. Translation of no. 323. Exists in various editions. (BL930.K2817 1810) DLC OCl *Great Britain*: BM *USSR*: LL (Slavic and Russian mythology)

323. Kaisarov, Andrei Sergeevich. *Versuch einer slavischer Mythologie in alphabetischer Ordnung*. Goettigen, 1804. 117 p. MH OCl See no. 322

324. Kalaidovich, I. "Perun," *Vestnik Evropy*, 1807, ch. 36, no. 24, pp 267-80. (Perun)

325. Kalina von Jaetenstein, Mathias. *Boehmens heidnische Opferplaetze, Graeber und Alterthuemer*. Prag, Gottlieb Haase Soehne, 1836. 252 p. CLU CU MH NIC OCl

326. Kaloianov, Ancho. *Bŭlgarski mitove.* Sofia, Nar. Mladezh, 1979. 242 p. (BL930.K29) DLC IU ViU WU (Bulgarian myth)

327. Kaneskii, K. "Veles, zabytoe istorieiu iazycheskoe bozhestvo sievernykh slavian," *Sievernaia pchela*, 1844, no. 162, p. 1. (Veles; the forogtten history of the pagan god of the northern Slavs)

328. Karbe, W. "Arkona-Rethra-Vineta," *Zeitschrift fuer slavische Philologie*, 2 (1925) pp 365-72.

329. Kareev, Nikolai Ivanovich. "Glavnye antropomorficheskie bogi slavianskogo iazychestva," *Filologicheskiia zapiski*, 1872, no. 3, pp 1-23, no. 4, pp 23-44, no. 5, pp 45-61. (The chief anthropomorphic gods of Slavic paganism) See no. 330

330. Kareev, Nikolai Ivanovich. *Glavnye antroopmorficheskie bogi slavianskogo iazychestva.* Voronezh, Tip. Gub. Prav., 1872. 61 p. *USSR*: LL (The chief anthropomorphic gods of Slavic paganism) See no. 329

331. Karger, Mikhail Konstantinovich. "Kapishche i voprosy ego rekonstruktsii." in his *Drevnii Kiev; ocherki po istorii material'noi kul'tury drevnerusskogo goroda.* Leningrad, Izd-vo ANSSSR, 1958-61. v. 1, pp 105-12. (DK651.K37K32) DLC CaBVaU CaOTU CLSU CLU CoU CSt CtW CtY CU CU-S DDO DeU FMU FU GU IaU ICRL ICU IEN InU IU KU LNHT LU MdU MH MiEM MiU MiU MNS MnU MoSW NBC NBuU NcGU NcU NIC NjP NjR NN NNC NRU OClW-H OCU OO OrU OU PPiU PPULC PU PU PU-MU RPB TNJ TU ViU VtU WaU OrU OU PPiU PPULC PU PU PU-MU RPB TNJ TU ViU VtU WaU WU   *Great Britain*: BM *USSR*: GPIB LL (The sanctuary and the questions of its reconstruction)

332. Karlowitz, Jan. "Germanische Elemente im slavischer Mythus und Brauch," *Archiv fuer Religionswissenschaft*, 3 (1900) pp 184-93.

333. Kastorksii, Mikhail Ivanovich. *Nachertanie slavianskoi mifologii.* St. Peterburg, V tip. E. Fishera, 1841. 182 p. CU KU MH MnU NN NNC OCl *Great Britain*: BM *USSR*: GPIB LL Reviewed in *Jahrbuecher fuer slawische Literatur, Kunst und Wissenschaft*, 1 (1843) no. 1, pp 64-8. (An outline of Slavic mythology)

334. Kellner, Peter. (Peter Z. Hostinský, pseud.) *Stará Viernauka Slovenská*, Pest, Minerva, 1872. 122 p. MH OCl (Old Slavic belief)

335. Kirfel, Willibald. "Dreikoepfige Gottheiten bei den Slaven." in his *Die Dreikoepfige Gottheit. Archaeologisch-etnologischer Steifzug durch die Ikonographie der Religionen.* Bonn, F. Duemmler, 1948.

pp 86-94. CaBVaU CLU CtY DDO ICU MH NIC NN NPurMC OrU OU PU

336. Kirpichnikov, Aleksandr Ivanovich. "Chto my znaem dostovernago o lichnykh bozhestvakh slavian," Russia. Ministerstvo narodnogo prosveshcheniia. *Zhurnal*, ch. 241 (1885) pp 47-65. (What we know for certain concerning the personal gods of the Slavs)

337. Kizilov, IU. A. "Evoliutsiia miroponimaniia i religioznykh predstavlenii pervobytnykh slavian." in *Voprosy istorii SSSR. Sbornik statei.* Ul'ianovsk, 1974. pp 62-77. IU *USSR*: LL (The evolution of the world view and the religious ideas of the primitive Slavs)

338. Kloeden, Karl Friederich. "Die Goetter des Wendenlandes und die Orte ihrer Verehrung," *Maerkische Forschungen*, 3 (1847) pp 193-291.

339. Knebel, J. "Arkona. Poslednja pohanska svjatnica zapadnych Słowjanow zniči so pred 800 lĕtami," *Rozhlad*, 19 (1969) no. 5, pp 176-84. (Arkona, the last pagan sanctuary of the Western Slavs, destroyed for 800 years)

340. Knebel, J. "Arkona. Poslednja pohanska swjatnica zapadnych Słowjanow zniči so pred 800 lĕtami," *Serbska pratyja*, 1970, pp 74-6. (Arkona, the last pagan sanctuary of the Western Slavs, destroyed for 800 years)

341. Knebel, J. "Na slĕdach swjatnicow Swarožiča a Swjatowita," *Serbska protyka*, 1969 pp 86-90. (On the trail of the sanctuaries of Swarozich and Swiatowit)

342. Knoop, O. "Zu Bĕlbog und Černobog," Verein fuer kaschubische Volkskunde, Karthaus. *Mitteilungen*, 1 (1908) no. 3, pp 98-100.

343. Knutsson, K. "Der Tempel in Arkona," *Zeitschrift fuer slavische Philologie*, 16 (1939) pp 141-51.

344. Kocha, L. A. "Drevnerusskoe iazychestvo." in *Istoriia i kul'tura slavianskikh stran. (Sbornik studench. nauch. rabot)* V.V. Mavrodin, ed. Leningrad, Izd-vo Leningradskogo un-ta, 1973. pp 1-9. (DR23.I84) DLC *USSR*: LL (Ancient Russian paganism)

345. Kocha, L. A. "Iazychestvo v drevnei Rusi." in *Sovetskaia istoriografiia Kievskoi Rusi.* V.V. Mavrodin, ed. Leningrad, Nauka, 1978. pp 166-71. (DK71.S67) DLC AzTeS AzU CtU CU-SB DDO GU ICIU InU IU MiEM NcGU NSyU OU RPB TU TxU ViBlbV ViU WaU WU *USSR*: LL (Paganism in Ancient Rus)

346. Kollar, Jan. "Die Goetter von Retra." in Český akademický spolek ve Vídni. *Jan Kollar 1793-1852.* Ve Vídni, Tiskem J. Otty v Praze, 1893. pp 243-6. (PG5038.K7Z55) DLC InU WU

347. Kollar Jan. *Sláwa bohyně.* Pest, Tiskem J.M. Trattner-Károlyiho, 1839. 358 p. (BL930.K6) DLC CSt CtY CU ICU MH NjP NN *Great Britain*: BM *USSR*: GPIB LL (Slavic gods)

348. Kondratov, A. "Bogi Kievskoi Rusi," *Nauka i religiia*, 1970, no. 6, pp 40-3. (The gods of Kiev Rus)

349. Korsh, Fedor Evgen'evich. *Vladimirovy bogi.* Khar'kov, Tip. "Pechatnoe Delo", 1908. 8 p. *USSR*: LL (Vladimir's gods) See no. 350

350. Korsh, Fedor Evgen'evich. "Vladimirovy bogi," Kharkov. Universytet. Istoriko-filologicheskoe obshchestvo. *Sbornik*, 18 (1909) no. 8, pp 51-8. (Vladimir's gods) See no. 349

351. Kortuem, J. CH. P. *Beschreibung eines neulich bey Neubrandenburg gefundenen wendischen Monuments mit historischen Erlaeuterungen zur naeheren Bestimmung der Lage des alten Rhetra.* Neubrandenburg, 1798. 45 p.

352. Kostomarov, Nikolai Ivanovich. "Nieskol'ko slov o slaviano-russkoi mifologii v iazycheskom periode, preimushchestvennoe v sviazi s narodnoiu poezieiu." in *Russkiia drevnosti.* V. Prokhorov, ed. St Petersburg, Tip. Akademii nauk, 1871-76. kn. 1, pp 1-24. InU IU NN OrU PPPM *Great Britain*: BM *USSR*: LL (A few words on Slavic-Russian mythology in the pagan period, in connection with folk poetry)

353. Kostomarov, Nikolai Ivanovich. "Nieskol'ko slov o slaviano-russkoi mifologii v iazycheskom periode, preimushchestvennoe v sviazi s narodnoiu poezieiu," *Khristianskiia drevnosti i arkheologiia*, 1872, no. 1, pp 1-24. (A few words on Slavic-Russian mythology in the pagan period, in connection with folk poetry)

354. Kostomarov, Nikolai Ivanovch. *Slavianskaia mifologiia.* Kiev, V Tip. I. Val'nera, 1847. 113 p. (BL930.K86) DLC CU NN NNC OCl *Great Britain*: BM *USSR*: GPIB Reprinted in London, 1978. (Slavic mythology)

355. Kotliarevskii, Aleksandr Aleksandrovich. *Skazaniia ob Ottone Bambergskom v otnoshenii slavianskoi istorii i drevnosti.* Praga, Tip. K.L. Klaudi, 1874. 160 p. (Series: Materialy dlia slavianskoi istorii i drevnosti) (DD491.P72K6) DLC CSt IaU OU WaU *Great Britain*: BM *USSR*: LL (Tales about Otto of Bamberg in relation to Slavic history and antiquity)

356. Kovalevskii, A. P. "Al'Masudi o slavianskikh iazycheskikh khramakh." in *Voprosy istoriografii i istochnikovedeniia slavianogermanskikh otnoshenii. Sbornik statei.* V.D. Koroliuk, ed. Moskva, Nauka, 1973. pp 80-86. (DR38.3G3V66) DLC CaBVaU CaOTU CLU CSt CSt-H CtY CU CU-SB DDO FMU ICIU ICU IEN InU IU MB MdU MH MiEM MiU MnU MoSW MoU MU NcU NIC NjP NN NNC OrU PSt RPB TNJ TxU ViU WaU WU *USSR*: GPIB LL (Al'Masudi on the Slavic pagan temples)

357. Kowalczyk, Małgorzata. *Wierzenia pogańskie za perwszych Piastów.* Łódź, Wydawn. Łódzkiej, 1968. 146 p. (BR934.K68) DLC CtY InU MB MH NjP *Great Britain*: BM *USSR*: ANSSSR-INION BLitSSR GBIL KievGU LGU LvovGB Reviewed in *Euhemer*, 14 (1970) no. 2, pp 132-34. (The pagan beliefs after the first Piasts)

358. Kozłowski, R. "Badania technologiczne posągu Światowita z museum archeologicznego w Krakowie," Krakow. Muzeum Archeologiczne. *Materiały archeologiczne*, 5 (1964) pp 61-7. French summary. (Technical research on the figure of Swiatowit from the archeological museum in Krakow)

359. Kramarek, Janusz. *Wierzenia dawnych Słowian.* Wrocław, 1968. 71 p. (Series: Museum archeologiczne we Wrocławiu. Biblioteka popularnauk, no. 3) *USSR*: ANSSSR-INION BANEst (The beliefs of the early Slavs)

360. Krappe, A. H. "La chute du paganisme à Kiev," *Revue des études slaves*, 17 (1937) pp 206-18.

361. Krauss, Friederich Salomo. *Volksglaube und religioeser Brauch der Suedslaven.* Muenster, Aschendorff, 1890. 176 p. (BL930.K7) DLC FU ICJ InU KAS KU MB MH MiU NcD NNUT OCl OClW OCU OU PU TxU UU *Great Britain*: BM *USSR*: GPIB (Reviewed in *Archiv fuer Religonswissenschaft*, 6 (1903) pp 92-3.

362. Kravtsiv, Bohdan. *Do problemi Tura-Svaroga-Troiana.* Philadelphia, America, 1952. 15 p. MH NN NSyU (Concerning the problem of Tur-Svarog-Troian)

363. Kravtsiv, Bohdan. "Mitolohiia ukrains'koi zemli." in *Istoriia ukrains'koi kul'tury.* I. Kryp'iakevych, ed. Vinnipeg, Kliub priiateli Ukr. Knizhki, 1964. v. 1, pp 15-28. (DK508.4I87) DLC CaOTU CtY ICIU ICU IU KU MB MH MiD NBuU NjP NSyU WaU (The mythology of the Ukrainian land)

364. Krek, Gregor. "Beitraege zur slavischen Mythologie," *Archiv fuer slavische Philologie*, 1 (1879) pp 134-51.

365. Kreussler, Heinrich Gottlieb. "Von den Oertern, wo die Sorben-wenden ueberhaupt, mamentlich aber in der Oberlausitz ihre Gottheiten verehrten, ihren Priestern und Festtagaen, ihren haeuslichen Einrichtungen und uebrigen Sitten und Gebraeu-chen." in his *Dess. Altsaechs. u. sorbenwend. Alterthuemer fuer die Jugend.* Leipzig, 1823, t. 1, pp 211-46.

366. Krolmus, Vaclav. *Posledni božíště Černoboha s runami na sklasku v kraji Boleslavskem v Čechách.* Praha, 1857. 48 p. (BL930.K76) DLC MH *Great Britain*: BM (Traces of the god Chernobog from runes on stones in the Boleslavski district in Bohemia)

367. Krueger, A. G. "Rethra und Arkona, die slavischen National-Heilig-tuemer in Norddeutschland," *Unser Pommerland*, 11 (1926) pp 180-4.

368. Krueger, A. G. "Rethra und Arkona. Die slavischen Nationalheilig-tuemer in Norddeutschland," *Mecklenburgische Monatshefte*, 2 (1926) pp 136-41.

369. Krueger, A. G. "Rethra und Arkona. Die slawischen Heiligtuemer in Deutschland," *Germanien*, 9 (1936) pp 264-72.

370. Kubalík, J. "Náboženství starých Slovanů," *Duchovní pastýr*, 9 (1961) pp 164-66. (The beliefs of the old Slavs)

371. Kuczyński, Janusz & Pyzik, Zygmunt Słodzimierz. "Ośrodek kultu pogańskiego na górze Grodowej w Tumline, pow. Kielce." in *Religia pogańskich Słowian; sesja naukowa w Kielcach.* Kielce, 1968. pp 61-67. (The center of a pagan cult on Gora Gordowa in Tumlin, Kelce district See no. 635

372. Kudláček, J. "Vývin náboženskych predstáv dávnych Slovanov," *Priroda a spoločnost'.* 5 (1956) pp 104-8. (The development of the religious ideas of the early Slavs)

373. Kulišic, Špiro. *Stara slovenska religija u svjetlu novijih istraživanja posebo balkanoloških.* Sarajevo, Akademija nauka i umjetnosti Bosne i Hercegovine, 1979. 246 p. InU OrU ViU WaU WU Reviewed in *Slavic Review*, 42 (1983) no. 2, pp 316-7. (Ancient Slavic religion in light of recent research, particularly Balkan)

374. Kurinnyi, P. "Sviatovit," *Vyzvol'nyi shliakh*, 6 (1954) pp 57-64. (Swiatowit)

375. Kuza, A. V. & Solov'eva, G. F. "Iazycheskoe sviatilishche v zemle radimichei," *Sovetskaia arkheologiia*, 1972, no. 1, pp 146-53. French summary. (The pagan sanctuary in the Radimich land)

376. Kvashnin-Samarin, N. "Ocherk slavianskoi mifologii," *Besieda*, 1872, no. 4, pp 219-68. (An essay on Slavic mythology)

377. Lasicki, Jan. *De Russorum, Moscovitarum et Tartarorum religione, sacrificiis, nuptiarum funerum ritu.* Spirae, 1582. 295 p. (BR932. A3L3) DLC MiU NMnU MoSU NN OCl OU PPamP *Great Britain*: BM *France*: BN

378. Laushkin, K. D. "Dereviannaia figurka antromorfnogo sushchestva iz Staroi Ladogi." in *Fol'klor i etnografiia russkogo severa.* B.N. Putilov & K.V. Chistov, eds., Leningrad, Nauka, 1973. pp 250-79. (GR203.N67F64) DLC AkU CaBVaU CaOTU CaQMM CLU CtY CU CU-SB ICU InLP InU IU MB MH MiDW MiEM MiU MnU MoU MU NcD NcU NhD NIC NjP NN NNC OrU PPiU PSt RPB TNJ TxU ViBlbV ViU WaU WU *USSR*: GPIB LL (A wooden human figure from Staraia Ladoga)

379. Laushkin, K. D. "Dereviannyi idol iz Staroi Ladogi," Akademiia nauk SSSR. Institut etnografii. Leningradskoe otdelenie. *Tezisy dokladov godichnoi nauchnoi sessii*, 1968, pp 71-2. (A wooden idol from Staraia Ladoga)

380. Lavrov, N. F. "Relgiiia i tserkov." in Akademiia nauk SSSR. Institut arkheologii. *Istorii kul'tury drevnei Rusi.* Moskva, Izd-vo AN-SSSR, 1948, v. 2, chapter 3, pp 61-113. (DK32.A37) Available from University Microfilms International. DLC CaOTU CLSU CLU CoU CSt-H CtY CU DS FU IaU ICU IEN MdBJ MH MiU MU NBC NcD NcU NjP NNC OU PSt RPB WaU *USSR*: GPIB LL (Religion and the Church)

381. Lavrovksii, Petr Alekseevich. "Razbor issledovaniia "O mificheskom znachenii nekotorykh poverii i obriadov A. Potebni," Moscow. Universitet. Obshchestvo istorii i drevnostei rossiskikh. *Chteniia*, 1866, April–June, pp 1-102. (An analysis of the "Mythical meaning of some beliefs and customs" by A. Potebna) See nos. 382, 542

382. Lavrovskii, Petr Alekseevich. *Razbor issledovaniia A. Potebni o mificheskom znachenii nekotorykh poverii i obriadov.* Moskva, 1866. 102 p. IU OCl *USSR*: LL (An analysis of the research of A. Potebna concerning the mythical meaning of some beliefs and customs) See nos. 381, 542

383. Lazowski, J. K. "Przedchrześcianskie na ziemi naszéj, pomniki dla bóstw Lelum Polelum i Świstum Poświstum," *Biblioteka warszawska*, 1844 no. 1, pp 211-3. (Pagans in our country; the monuments for the gods Lelum Polelum and Swistum Poswistum)

384. Ledić, Franjo. *Mitologija slavena.* Zagreb, Franjo Ledić, 1969-70. (BL930.L37) DLC CaBVaU CLU CSt CtY CU ICU IU MH MiEM MiU MU NjP NN NNC NSyU WaU WU *USSR*: LL (Slavic mythology)

385. Le Fevre, Andre Paul Emile. "Mythologie des Slaves et des Finnois," *Revue anthropologique*, 7 (1897) pp 225-47.

386. Leger, Louis Paul Marie. *Esquisse sommaire de la mythologie slave.* Paris, E. Leroux, 1883. 24 p. CU KU OCl

387. Leger, Louis Paul Marie. "Etude de mythologie slave," *Revue de l'histoire des religions*, 31 (18950 pp 89-102, 33 (1896) pp 1-18, 38 (1898) pp 123-55, 39 (1899) pp 1-17.

388. Leger, Louis Paul Marie. *Études de mythologie slave.* Paris, Maisonneuve, 1895-97. 3 parts. I. *Peroun et les Saint Elie.* iI. *Svantovit et les dieux en "vit".* III. *L'Empereur Trajan dans la mythologie slave. France:* BN Reviewed in *Kwartalnik historyczny*, 13 (1899) pp 84-5.

389. Leger, Louis Paul Marie. *Études de mythologie slave. Les divinites inferieures.* Paris, E. Leroux, 1898. 15 p. *France:* BN

390. Leger, Louis Paul Marie. *La Mythologie slave.* Paris, E. Leroux, 1901. 248 p. (BL930.L4) DLC CtY DDO ICJ MH MiU NN OCl PU WU *USSR*: GPIB Reviewed in Prague. Národní museum. Časopis, 75 (1901) pp 390-1.

391. Leger, Louis Paul Marie. "Slavianskaia mifologiia," *Filologicheskiia zapiski*, 1907, vyp. 2-3, pp 1-65. vyp. 4, pp 65-100, vyp. 5-6, pp 101-91. (Slavic mythology)

392. Leger, Louis Paul Marie. "Slovanske mythologii," *Slovanský sborník*, 2 (1883) pp 390-4, 440-6. (Slavic mythology)

393. Leger, Louis Paul Marie. *Slovenska mitologija.* U Beogradu, Shtampano u stampariji D. Dimitrijevića, 1904. 245 p. IU (Slavic mythology)

394. Leger, Louis Paul Marie. "Les sources de la mythologie slave," *Revue de l'histoire des religions*, 33 (1896) pp 273-87, 35 (1897) pp 163-77.

395. Łegowski-Nadmorski, Józef. "Bóstwa i wierzenia religijne Słowian Lechickich," Towarzystwo naukowe w Toruniu. *Roczniki*, 32 (1925) pp 18-102. (The gods and religious beliefs of the western Slavs)

396. Łegowksi-Nadmorski, Józef. "Słowianskie bóstwa Białybóg, Strzybóg, Lutybóg i Piorun w dokumentach Pomorskich," Towarzystwo naukowe w Toruniu. Wydział nauk historycznych, prawniczych i społecznych. *Zapiski*, 4 (1917) no. 1, pp 2-10. (The Slavic gods Belobog, Stribog, Lutybog and Perun in Pomeranian documents)

397. Leicht, Pier, Silverio. "Tracce di paganesimo fra gli Sclavi dell'Isonzo nel secolo XIV," *Studi e materiali di storia delle religioni*, 1 (1925) pp 247-50.

398. Lelekov, L. A. "K rekonstruktsii ranneslavianskoi mifologicheskoi sistemy," *Sovetskoe slavianovedenie*, 1973, no. 1, pp 52-9. (Concerning the reconstruction of the early Slavic mythological system)

399. Lelewel, Joachim. *Bałwochwastwo sławiańskie*. Poznan, J.K. Żupanski, 1853. 37 p. NN *Great Britain*: BM (Slavic paganism)

400. Lelewel, Joachim. *Cześć bałwochwalcza Słowianie*. Poznan, J.K. Żupanski, 1855. 128 p. (BL930.L45) DLC NN (The pagan worship of the Slavs)

401. Leńczyk, G. "A jednak autentyczny i Słowiański," *Z otchłani wieków*, 1965, no. 1, pp 9-17. (And yet authentic and Slavic (re Zbruch idol)

402. Leńczyk, G. "Świtowid Zbruczanski," Krakow. Muzeum archeologiczne. *Materiały archeologiczne*, 5 (1964) pp 5-61. French summary. (The Zbruch Swiatowit)

403. Leśny, Jan. "W sprawie kultu pogańskiego na ostrowie lednickim we wczesnym średniowieczu," *Slavia antiqua*, 21 (1974) pp 119-35. French summary. (In regard to the pagan cult on the western islands in the early Middle Ages)

404. Lettenbauer, W. "Deutsche Forschungen zur slawischen Religionsgeschichte," *Archiv fuer Religionswissenschaft*, 37 (1941-42) pp 174-82.

405. Leube, Achim. "Schutz und Erhaltung der slawischen Tempelburg Arkona auf Ruegen," *Altertum*, 22 (1976) no. 3, pp 141-8.

406. Liebusch, Georg. *Skythika, oder etymologische und kritische Bemerkungen ueber alte Bergreligion und spaetern Fetischimus, mit besonderer Beruecksichtigugn der slavischen Voelker und Goetternamen*. Camenz, gedruckt bei C.S. Krausche, 1833. 321 p. CtY ICU MH NcD *Great Britain*: BM *France*: BN *USSR*: GPIB

407. Lippert, Julius. "Die Religion der Slaven." in his *Die Religionen der europaeischen Culturvoelker, der Litauer, Slaven, Germanen, Griechen und Roemer, in ihrem geschichtlichen Ursprunge.* Berlin, T. Hofmann, 1881. pp 68-114. CtY CU DDO ICU InU MB NcD NIC NjP OCl OClW PU *Great Britain*: BM *USSR*: LL

408. Lisch, G. C. F. "Ueber den wendischen Goetzen und die Stadt Goderac," *Mecklenburgische Jahrbuecher*, 6 (1841) pp 70-8.

409. Lisch, G. C. F. "Ueber die wendische Stadt Goderak," *Mecklenburgische Jahrbuecher*, 21 (1856) pp 51-4.

410. Lisch, G. C. F. "Der wendische Goetze Goderac und der heilige Gotthart," *Mecklenburgische Jahrbuecher*, 13 (1848) pp 242-3.

411. Livesay, F. R. & Crath, Paul. "Religion of the ancient Ukraine in the light of archaeology and folklore," *Scientific American supplement*, 85 (1918) pp 114-5.

412. Ljapunov, "Blasios-Volos," *Archiv fuer slavische Philologie*, 9 (1886) pp 315-6.

413. Loehn, E. W. "Andeutungen zu einer keunftigen Bearbeitung der Mythologie der Polaben," *Zeitschrift fuer die historische Theologie*, 1845, pp 69-97.

414. Loehn, E. W. "Andeutungen zu einer kuenftigen Bearbeitung der Mythologie der polabischen Sorben," *Zeitschrift fuer die historische Theologie*, 1848, pp 515-71.

415. Longinov, A. V. "Slovo o polku Igoreve (istochniki i mifologiia "Slova." Ego nauchnoe i vospitatel'noe znachenie)," Odesskoe obshchestvo istorii i drevnostei. *Zapiski*, 29 (1911) pp 45-116. (The Slovo o polku Igoreve) (Sources and mythology of the Slovo. Its scientific and educational meaning.)

416. Lorentz, F. "Belbog und Cernobog," Verein fuer kaschubische Volkskunde, Karthaus. *Mitteilungen*, 1 (1908) pp 19-23.

417. Loukine, Rostislas. *Mythologie russe.* Bruxelles, Totradim, 1946. 54 p. (BL930.L6) DLC NN NNC OCl

418. Łowmiański, Henryk. *Religia Słowian i jej upadek (w. VI-XII).* Warszawa, Państwowe Wydawnictwo Naukowe, 1979. 433 p. (BL930.L64) DLC InU IU KU MH MiDW NBuU NcU OU ViU WaU WU (The religion of the Slavs and its decline during the sixth to twelfth centuries)

419. Lubicz, L. A. *Mitologia słowiańska podług Naruszewicza, Lelewela, Bogusławskiego, Bruecknera i Grusszewskiego.* Warszawa, Wydawnictwo M. Arcta, 1911. 182 p. OCl (Slavic mythology according to Naruszewicz, Lelewel, Bogusławski, Brueckner and Grusszewski)

420. Luecke, G. "Flinz—der Wendenabgott," *Bautzener Geschichtshefte,* 2 (1924) no. 2, pp 1-15.

421. Łuka, Leon Jan. *Wierzenia pogańskie na pomorzu wschodnim w starożytności i we wczesnym średniowieczu.* Gdańsk, Zakł. Narodowy im. Ossolińskich, 1973. 89 p. (Series: Muzeum archeologiczne w Gdańsku. Zeszyty popularnaukowe, no. 2) (GN845.P7L84) DLC OU *USSR*: LL Reviewed in *Slavia antiqua,* 18 (1976) pp 323-5. (Pagan beliefs in eastern Pomerania in antiquity and in the early Middle Ages)

422. Machal, Jan. *Bájesloví slovanské.* Praha, Nákl. J. Otty, 1907. 174 p. CU InU MB MiU (Slavic folklore)

423. Machal, Jan. *Nákres slovanského bájesloví.* Praha, F. Šimáček, 1891. 221 p. (GR157.M2) DLC CSt CtY InU IU KU MB MHMiU McU NN OU PSt UU Reviewed in *Archiv fuer slavische Philologie,* 17 (1895) pp 583-9. (An outline of Slavic folklore)

424. Machal, Jan. "O lužické modle Flins," *Slovanský sborník,* 3 (1884) pp 285-90. (Concerning the Lusatian idol Flins)

425. Machal, Jan. "Slavic mythology," in *The Mythology of All Races.* Boston, Marshall Jones Co., 1918, v. 3, pp 253-69. Exists in various editions. (BL25.M99) DLC CaBVaU CU ICJ ICN MB MH MH-AH MiU NB NIC NN OCl OCU OU PU TxU

426. Machal, Jan. "Vrchy Běloboh a Čornoboh v Lužici," *Slovanský sborník,* 4 (1885) pp 393-7. (The appearance of Belobog and Chernobog in Lusatia)

427. Machek, Vaclav. "Essai comparatif sur la mythologie slave," *Revue des études slaves,* 23 (1947) pp 48-65.

428. Machek, Vaclav. "Slav. Rarog 'Wuerzfalke' und sein mythologischer Zusammenhang," *Linguistica slovaca,* 3 (1941) pp 84-8.

429. Machek, Vaclav. "Die Stellung des Gottes Svantovit in der altslavischen Religion." in Gerhardt, Dietrich. *Orbis Scriptus: Festschrift fuer Dmitrij Tschizewskij zum 70. Geburtstag.* Munich, W. Fink, 1966, pp 491-7. (PG14.C52) DLC CaBVaU CLSU CLU CoU

CSt CtY CU CU-S DDO IaU ICU KU LNHT MdU MH MiDW
MiEM MiU MnU MoSW NBC NbU NBuU NIC NjP NmU NN
NRU NSyU OO OrU OU PPiU PPULC RPB TNJ TxHR TxU
UU ViU VtMiM WaU WU *France*: BN *USSR*: SS

430. Machnik, Jan. "Na śladach kultu Peruna," *Dawna kultura*, 2 (1955)
no. 3, pp 144-7. (On the trail of Perun's cult)

431. Machnik, Jan. "Nowe odkrycie posągów kamiennych w ZSSR," *Z otchłani wieków*, 22 (1953) no. 6, pp 249-50. (Newly discovered stone statues in the USSR)

432. Maciejowski, W. A. "Wzglad na zabytki pogaństwa w Polsce," *Athenaeum*, 3 (1843) no. 1, pp 7-16. (Considering the pagan relics in Poland)

433. Mal, Josip. "Contributi alla mitologia slovena," *Studi e materiali di storia delle religioni*, 18 (1942) pp 20-35.

434. Mal, Josip. "Pripombe k slovenskemu bajeslovju," *Slovenski etnograf*, 5 (1952) pp 251-56. (An observation concerning Slavic folklore)

435. Mal, Josip. "Slovenske mitološke starine," Muzejsko društvo za Slovenijo, Ljubljana. *Glasnik*, 21 (1940) pp 1-37. (Slavic mythological antiquities) See no. 436.

436. Mal, Josip. *Slovenske mitološke starine*. Ljubljana, 1940. 37 p. CaBVaU (Slavic mythological antiquities) See no. 435

437. Mansikka, Viljo Johannes. *Die Religion der Ostslaven*. Helsinki, Soumalainen tiedeakatemia, 1922. 408 p. (Series: Folklore Fellows Communications, v. 10 no. 43) (GR1.F55 no. 43) DLC DDO GU MiU MoU NN OCl OU UU *USSR*: GPIB LL Reviewed in *Slavia*, 2 (1923-24) pp 527-47, 765-78.

438. Maretic, Tomislav. "Zu den Goetternamen der baltischen Slaven," *Archiv fuer slavische Philologie*, 10 (1887) pp 133-42.

439. Martyniuk, Ivan. "Do istorii narodnykh viruvan'," *Vyzvol'nyi shliiakh*, 30 (1977) no. 9, pp 1057-68. (The history of folk belief)

440. Masch, Andreas Gottlieb. *Die gottesdienstlichen Alterthuemer der Obstriten aus dem Tempel zu Rhethra*. Berlin, Gedruckt bei Carl Friedrich Rellsrab, 1771. 151 p. *Great Britain*: BM *France*: BN *German Democratic Republic*: GLB *USSR*: LL

441. Masch, G. M. C. "Die prillwitzer Goetzenbilder," *Mecklenburgische Jahrbuecher*, 3 (1838) p. 190.

442. Masius, Hector Gottfried. *Hect. Gothofr. Masii, Mecklenburgensis. Antiquitatum Mecklenburgensium schediasma historico-philologicum.* Lubecae, Apud J. Wiedmeyerum, 1700. 166 p. (DD801.M345M3) DLC MH MnU NjP *German Democratic Republic*: GLB First published under the title *Schediasma historico-philologicum de diis obotritis seu idolis Mecklenburgensium & praecipue de Radegasto.* Copenhagen, J.P. Bockenhoffer, 1688. 166 p. *USSR*: GPIB LL

443. Matić, Vojin. *Psihoanaliza mitske prošlosti.* Beograd, Prosveta, 1976. 228 p. (GN508.M37) DLC CaBVaU IU MH NjP (A psychoanalysis of the mythical past)

444. Matusiak, Szymon. "Olimp polski podług Dlugosza," *Lud,* 14 (1908) pp 19-89, 205-35. (The Polish Olympus according to Długosz)

445. Matusiak, Szymon. "Piorun a Perkun," *Lud,* 14 (1908) pp 199-201. (Thunder and Perun)

446. Matusiak, Szymon. "Tria idola na Łysej Górze," *Lud* 14 (1908) no. 4, pp 313-26. (Three idols on Lysa Gora)

447. Maury, Louis Ferdinand Alfred. "Essai historique sur la religion des Aryas pour servir a éclairer les origines des religions hellénique, latine, gaulois, germaine et slave," *Revue archéologique,* ser. 1, 9 (1852) pp 589-616, 717-35, 10 (1853) pp 1-13, 129-50. See no. 448

448. Maury, Louis Ferdinand Alfred. *Essai historique sur la religion des Aryas pour servir a éclairer les origines des religions hellénique, latine, gaulois, germaine et slave.* Paris, 1853. 77 p. *France*: BN See no. 447

449. Menges, K. H. "Early Slavo-Iranian contacts and Iranian influences in Slavic mythology." in *60. doğum yili münasebetiyle Zeki Velidi Togańa armanagan. Symbolae in honorem Z.V. Togan.* Istanbul, 1950-55. pp 468-79. (PJ26.T6) DLC CLU ICU PU

450. Meriggi, B. "Il concetto del Dio nelle religioni dei populi slavi," *Ricerche slavistiche,* 1 (1952) pp 148-76.

451. Meriggi, B. "Unus Deus" di Helmold." in his *Scritti minori.* Brescia, 1975. pp 141-51. (PG13.M4) DLC CtY IU NcU

452. Metlewicz, J. "O Swietym Wicie i Światowicie," *Biblioteka warszawska,* 4 (1845) p 335. (Concerning the holy council and Swiatowit)

453. Meulen, Reinder van der. *De Godsdienst der heidensche Balten en Slaven.* Baarn, Hollandia-Druckkerij, 1913. n.p. (Series: Groote Godsdiensten, ser. 2, no. 10) OCl

454. Meulen, Reinder van der. "De Godsdiensten der Slaven en Balten." in Leeuw, Gerardus van der. *De Godsdiensten der Wereld.* Amsterdam, H. Meulenhoff, 1955. pp 544-62. Exists in various editions. (BL80.L432 1948) DLC CtY ICU MH-AH OrU OU ViU

455. Meyer, Karl H. "Slavic religion." in Clemen, Carl. *Religions of the World.* New York, Harcourt, Brace & Co., 1931. pp 243-53. (BL80.C66) DLC CtY MB MH-AH MiU NcD NN OCl PPULC PU *Great Britain:* BM

456. Meyer, Karl H. "Die slavische Relgion." in Clemen, Carl. *Die Religionen der Erde.* Munich, F. Bruckmann, 1927. pp 261-72. Exists in various editions. (BL80.C65) DLC ICU PPULC RPB

457. Meyer, Karl H. "Vom Kult der Goetter und Geister in slawischer Urzeit," *Prace filologiczne,* 15 (1931) no. 2, pp 454-64.

458. Miller, M. "Pohanski bohu v Ukrajiny," *Novi Dni,* 1957, no. 87, pp 18-20, no. 93, pp 17-19. (Pagan gods in the Ukraine)

459. Mironchikov, L. T. "Dokhristianskie bogi vostochnykh slavian," *Voprosy istorii. Mezhvuzovskii sbornik,* vyp. 3 (1977) pp 79-88. (Pre-Christian gods of the Eastern Slavs)

460. Mironchikov, L. T. *Dokhristianskoe zhrechestvo drevnei Rusi (startsy, starosty, volkhvy).* Avtoreferat dissertatsii. Minsk, 1969. 26 p. *USSR:* LL (The pre-Christian priesthood of ancient Rus') See no. 461

461. Mironchikov, L. T. "Dokhristianskoe zhrechestov drevnei Rusi (startsy, starosty, volkhvy)," Dissertation. Minsk, 1969. 198 p. *USSR:* LL (The pre-Christian priesthood of ancient Rus') See no. 460

462. Mironchikov, L. T. "K voprosu periodizatsii drevnerusskogo iazychestvo po "Slovu Girgoriia." in *Tezisy dokladov respublikanskoi nauchnoi konferentsii molodykh uchenykh i aspirantov.* Minsk, 1968. pp 158-66. *USSR:* LL (Concerning the periodization of ancient Russian paganism according to Slovo Grigoriia)

463. Mironova, V. G. "Iazycheskoe zhertvoprinoshenie v Novgorode," *Sovetskaia arkheologiia,* 1967, no. 1, pp 215-27. (Pagan sacrifice in Novgorod)

464. "Mitologia słowiański," *Przyjaciel ludzi,* 3 (1836) no. 1, pp 11-12. (Slavic mythology)

465. Mlynek, L. "Zarys pierwotny religii Lachow," *Lud* 5 (1899) pp 53-6 (An outline of the primitive religion of the Lachs)

466. Mochulskii, Vasilii Nikolaevich. "O mnimom dualizme i mifologii slavian," *Russkii filologicheskii vestnik*, 21 (1889) pp 153-204. (Concerning the imaginary dualism and the mythology of the Slavs)

467. Moepert, A. "Die 'unbekannten Goetter' der rugischen Wenden," *Unser Pommerland*, 3 (1915-16) pp 193-8.

468. Mone, Franz Joseph. *Geschichte des Heidentums im noerdlichen Europa. I. Die Religionen der finnishcen, slawischen und skandinavischen Voelker.* Leipzig und Darmstadt, 1822. 479 p. IU KMK MH NIC NN *France*: BN *USSR*: GPIB

469. Moszyński, Kazimierz. *Kultura ludowa słowian.* Warszawa, Polska Akademja Umiejętności, 1934-37. 2v. Exists in various editions. (CB231.M6) DLC CaBVaU CSt CtY CU IU MoU NcU NjP NN OU PU WU *Great Britain*: BM Reviewed in *Lud*, 38 (1948) pp 314-8. (The culture of the Slavic people)

470. Mouravieff, Boris. "Des croyances slaves pré-chrétiennes," *Synthèses*, 161 (1959) pp 226-41.

471. Mučink, B. "Uebr den slavischen Abgott Flins," *Zeitschrift fuer slavische Literatur, Kunst und Wissenschaft*, 1 (1862-64) pp 261-7.

472. Mueller, Ewald. "Die Religion der alten Wenden." in his *Das Wendentum in der Niederlausitz.* Cotibus, 1922. pp 5-13. DLC-P4 IU RPB

473. Mueller, Hanns-Hermann. "Tieropfer fuer Swantewit in der slawischen Tempelburg von Arkona auf Ruegen," *Altertum*, 22 (1976) no. 2, pp 118-22.

474. Mueller, Hans-Hermann. "Vor 1000 Jahren: Tieropfer fuer den Slawengott Swantewit," *Urania*, 1975, no. 9, pp 14-7.

475. Nagy, Gregory. "Perkunas and Perun." in *Antiquitates Indogermanicae. Studien zur indogerman. Altertumskunde u. zur Sprach- u. Kulturgeschichte d. indogerman. Voelker.* Innsbruck, Inst. f. Sprachwissenschaft d. Univ. Innsbruck, 1974. pp 113-31. (Series: Innsbrucker Beitraege zur Sprachwissenschaft Bd. 12) (GN539. A57) DLC CLU CSt CU CU-SB GU IaU InU IU KyU MB MH MiDW MnU MoSW NBuU NIC NjP NN NNC OU PSt TxU ViU WU *USSR*: ANSSSR-INION LL

476. Nedo, P. "Czorneboh und Bieleboh. Zwei angebliche slawische Kultstaetten in der Oberlausitz," Bautzen, Germany. Institut za serbski ludospyt. *Letopis instituta za serbski ludospyt. Rjad C: Ludoweda*, no. 67/7 (1963-64) pp 5-18.

477. Nehring, Wladyslaw. "Der Name belbog in der slavischen Mythologie," *Archiv fuer slavische Philologie*, 25 (1903) pp 66-73.

478. Niederle, Lubor. "Arkona, Rethra, Redigast," *Slavia*, 2 (1923-24) pp 675-79.

479. Niederle, Lubor. *Manuel de l'antiquité slave*. Paris, E. Champion, 1926. 2v. (D147.N5) DLC CaBVaU CU DDO GU IaU ICU KU MH MiU NcD NcU NN NSyU OCl OCU OU PSt PU ViU *Great Britain*: BM *France*: BN Reviewed in *Zeitschrift fuer slavische Philologie*, 2 (1925) pp 539-43.

480. Niederle, Lubor. "Rethra a Arkona," *Obzor praehistorický*, 1 (1922) no. 2, pp 104-6. (Rethra and Arkona)

481. Niederle, Lubor. *Rukovět' slovanských starožitnoscí*. Praha, Nakl. Československé Akademie Věd. 1953. 513 p. (D147.N512) DLC CaBVaU CU DDO ICU IU MH NcD NcU NSyU ViU *Great Britain*: BM (Handbook of Slavic antiquities)

482. Niederle, Lubor. "Schuchhardtova Rethra," *Obzor praehistorický*, 2 (1923) no. 2, pp 124-5. (Schuchhardt's Rethra)

483. Niederle, Lubor. *Slovanské starožitnosti*. Praha, Bursík a Kohout, 1902– Exists in various editions. (D147.N55) DLC CaBVaU CU DDO ICJ ICU MB MH MiU NN NNC NSyU OCl ViU WaU *Great Britain*: BM Reviewed in *Slavia*, 2 (1923-24) pp 765-78. (Slavic antiquities)

484. Niederle, Lubor. "Un travail nouveau sur la mythologie russe," *Revue des études slaves*, 3 (1923) pp 115-20.

485. Niederle, Lubor. *Život starých Slovanů*. Praha, Nakl. Bursíka a Kohouta, 1911-34. 3v in 5. Exists in various editions. ICJ MH NIC WaU (The life of the ancient Slavs)

486. Niemeyer, J. F. *Mythologie der Griechen, Roemer, Aegypter, Norlaender, Wenden und Slawen*. Leipzig, O. Wigand, 1855. 415 p.

487. Nikiforovskii, M. *Russkoe iazychestvo*. St. Petersburg, 1875. 125 p. (BL930.N55) DLC NN *USSR*: GPIB LL (Russian paganism)

488. Nikol'skii, Nikolai Mikhailovich. *Dokhristianskie verovaniia i kul'ty dneprovskikh slavian*. Moskva, Ateist, 1929. 36 p. InU MiU NN *USSR*: GPIB LL Excerpt from his *Istoriia russkoi tserkvi*. Moskva, Ateist, 1930. 248 p. (BX485.N5) DLC ICU IU NcU NIC NN OU WU *USSR*: GPIB LL (Pre-Christian beliefs and cults of the Dnepr Slavs)

489. Nodilo, Natko. "Religija Srba i Hrvata," Jugoslovenska akademija znanosti i umjetnosti, Zagreb. *Rad*, 77 (1885) pp 185-246 81 (1886) pp 147-217, 84 (1887) pp 100-179, 85 (1887) pp 121-201, 89 (1888) pp 129-209, 91 (1888) pp 181-221, 94 (1889) pp 115-198, 99 (1890) pp 129-184, 101 (1890) pp 68-126. (The religion of Serbia and Croatia)

490. Nowak-Horjanski, J. "Přehled serbskeje mythologije," *Lužica*, 5 (1886) pp 69-71, 80, 84, 94. (A survey of Sorbic mythology)

491. "O bor'be khristianstva s iazychestvom v Rossii," *Pravoslavnyi sobesiednik*, 1865, ch. 2, pp 211-302. (Concerning the struggle of Christianity with Paganism in Russia)

492. "O mifologii," *Vestnik Evropy*, 1819, ch. 107, no. 18, pp 108-30. (Concerning mythology)

493. "O mitologii dawnych Słowianie," *Lech*, 1 (1823) pp 5-15, 33-8. (Concerning the mythology of the anicnet Slavs)

494. "Ocherki iz istorii slavianskoi mifologii," *Nizhegorodskiia eparkhial'nyia viedomosti*, 1865, no. 17, pp 22-36, no. 18, pp 9-32, no. 19, pp 24-32, no. 20, pp 9-21, no. 21, pp 22-32, 1866, no. 1, pp 9-24, no. 2, pp 51-62, no. 3, pp 107-16, no. 4, pp 156-68, no. 6, pp 229-44, no. 7, pp 279-86, no. 8, pp 309-21, no. 13, pp 511-37, no. 14, pp 561-81, no. 16, pp 236-44. (Essays from the history of Slavic mythology)

495. Oguibenine, Boris. "Le dieu Jazomir," *Wiener Slavistischer Almanach*, 4 (1979) pp 433-8.

496. Oppeln-Bronikowski, F. "Arkona, Rethra, Vineta," *Ostmecklenburgische Heimat*, 5 (1932) pp 2-5.

497. Osięgłowski, Janislaw. "Poczatki słowiańskiej Rugii do r. 1168," *Materiały zachodnio-pomorskie*, 13 (1967) pp 239-85. German summary. (Slavic Ruegen, from its origins to 1168)

498. Osięgłowski, Janislaw. "Upadek świętej wyspy," *Mówią wieki*, 10 (1967) no. 11, pp 1-4. (The fall of the holy island)

499. Osięgłowski, Janislaw. *Wyspa słowiańskich bogow*. Warszawa, Ksiązka i Wiedza, 1971. 326 p. (DD491.R950084) DLC CtY FU InU IU MH MiEM MU NjP WU *USSR*: ANSSSR-INION GPIB LErm LGU LvovGU VilGU Reviewed in *Z otchłani wieków*, 1971, no. 4, p 316. (The island of the Slavic gods)

500. Otrębski, J. "Slav. Svarog," *Die Welt der Slaven*, 16 (1971) no. 2, pp 151-54.

501. Otto, R. "Mythus und Religion nach wendischen Wundt," *Deutsche Literaturzeitung*, 1910, no. 31, pp 2373-82.

502. Palm, Thede. *Wendische Kultstaetten; quellenkritische Untersuchungen zu den letzen Jahrhunderten slavischen Heidentums.* Lund, Gleerupska Universitetbokhandeln, 1937. 179 p. (BL935.W4P3 1937) DLC CtY DDO NjP *Great Britain*: BM

503. Pascal, P. "La Religion des ancients slaves." in *Histoire des religions.* Paris, Bloud et Gay, 1953-57. v. 3, pp 89-103. (BL80.H48) DLC CU InU IU NNC TxU

504. Paul, Karel, "P. Jos. Šafařík a slovanská mythologie." in Narodopisná společnost českoslovanská, Prague. *Sborník prací věnovaných profesoru dru. Václav Tillovi k šedesátým narozeninám 1867-1927.* Praha, Nkl. Orbis, 1927. pp 149-58. InU MH TxU *USSR*: LL (P.J. Safarik and Slavic mythology)

505. Paulíny, Tóth, Viliam. *Slovenské bájeslovie.* Turčiansky Sv. Martin, Tlačou Kníhtlačiarkso-Účastinar Spolku, 1876. 109 p. (BL935. S6P3) DLC CLU ICU MH NNC OClW TxU (Slavic folklore)

506. Pavlovich, Boris Antonovich. *O iazycheskoi vere nashikh predkov i o tom, kak zadumal kniaz' Vladimir krestit'sia.* St. Petersburg, Naein i Merkul'ev, 1872. 25 p. *USSR*: GPIB (Concerning the pagan belief of our ancestors and how Prince Vladimir planned to be baptized)

507. Peisker, Johann. "Koje su vjere bili stari Sloveni prije krštenja?" Starohravatska prosvjeta. *Knih*, N.S. 2 (1928) pp 1-36. (What were the beliefs of the ancient Slavs prior to Christianity?) See no. 508

508. Peisker, Johann. *Koje su vjere bili stari Sloveni prije krštenja?* Zagreb, 1928. 36 p. DLC-P4 WaU (What were the beliefs of the ancient Slavs prior to Christianity?) See no. 507

509. Pełka, Leonard. *U stóp słowiańskiego parnasu.* Warszawa, Wydawn. Ministerwa Obrony Narodowej, 1960. 220 p. (BL930.P4) DLC OU *USSR*: ANSSSR-INION LL Lvov GU (At the foot of the Slavic Parnassus)

510. Petr, Viacheslav Ivanovich. "Ob etimologicheskom znachenii slova "Stribog" v sviazi indiiskim Sarameem i grecheskim Germesom." in *Izbornik Kievskii. Sbornik izdan po povodu 25-letiia nauchnoi i lit. deiatel'nosti T.D. Florinskogo.* Kiev, Tip. T.G. Meinandera, 1904, pp 106-18. (AC65.I9) DLC *USSR*: LL Available from University Microfilms International. (Concerning the etymolog-

ical meaning of the word "Stribog" in connection with the Indian Saram and the Greek Hermes)

511. Petrov, V. P. "Nazvi slov'ians'kikh (davn'orus'kikh) bozhestv." in Ukrains'ka Slavistychnà Konferentsiia, 6th, Chernivtsi, 1964. *Tezi dopovidei.* Chernivtsi, 1964. pp 169-70. *USSR*: LL (The names of the Slavic (early Russian) gods)

512. Petrovic, P. Z. "O perunovu kul'tu kod juznikh Slovena," Srpska akademija nauk i umetnosti, Belgrad. Etnografski Institut. *Glasnik*, 1-2 (19520 pp 373-80. German summary. (Concerning Perun's cult among the southern Slavs)

513. Petrushevich, Antonii Stepanovich. "Blizshoe izvestie o vremeni i mestnosti otkrytiia kamennogo istukan Sviatovida v ritsie Zbruche 1848 goda," Galitsko-russkaia matitsa, Lvov. *Nauchno-literaturnyi sbornik*, 1886, vyp. 1, pp 31-5. (Recent news about the time and place of the discovery of the stone statue of Swiatowit in the river Zbruch in 1848)

514. Petrushevich, Antonii Stepanovich. "O kamennom istukane Khorsa, Dazhd'boga, otkrytom v rusle reki Zbrucha v 1858 g.," Galitsko-russkaia matitsa, Lvov. *Naucho-literaturnyi sbornik*, 1885, vyp. 1, pp 1-7, vyp. 2-3, pp 73-111. (Concerning the stone state of Khors Dazhbog found in the channel of the Zbuch river in 1851)

515. Pettazzoni, Raffaele. "Osservazioni sul paganesimo degli Slavi occidentali," *Studi e material di storia delle religioni* 19-20 (1943-46) pp 157-69. For English translation, see no. 520

516. Pettazzoni, Raffaele. "The pagan origins of the three-headed representation of the Christian Trinity," London. University. Warburg Institute. *Journal*, 6 (1946) pp 135-51.

517. Pettazzoni, Raffaele. "La progenie del Sole," Brussels. Université libre. Institut de philologie et d'histoire orientales et slaves. *Annuaire*, 10 (1950) pp 493-500.

518. Pettazzoni, Raffaele. *La religione dei popoli slavi, secondo le testimonianze medievali greche e latine,* Roma, Edizioni Italiane, 194–124 p. (Series: Rome. Universita. Facolta di lettere e filosofia. Corsi, 18) CtY ICU NNUT

519. Pettazzoni, Raffaele. "The Slavs." in his *The All Knowing God.* London, Methuen, 1956. pp 234-55. (BL85.P433) DLC CU IaU ICU InU IU KyU LU MiU MoSW NcD OCl OrU RPB TxU WU

520. Pettazzoni, Raffaele. "West Slavic paganism." in his *Essays on the history of religion.* Leiden, Brill 1954. pp 151-63. (Series: Studies in the hsitory of religions; supplements to Numen, 1) (BL89.P38) DLC CaBVaU CtY IU MB MoU NIC NN OCl OClW OrU ViU Translation of no. 515

521. Petzsch, W. & Martiny, G. "Wall und Tor der Tempelfeste Arkona," *Praehistorische Zeitschrift,* 21 (1930) pp 237-64.

522. Pietkiewicz, Czeslaw. "Bóstwa rolnicze w wierzeniach białorusinow," *Wiadomości ludoznawcze,* 2 (1933) pp 14-21. (Agricultural gods in the beliefs of the Belorussians)

523. Pilar, Ivo. "O dualizmu u vjeri starih Slovjena i o njegovu podrijetlui znacenju," *Zbornik za narodni život i običaje južnih Slovena,* 28 (1931) pp 1-86. (Concerning the dual beliefs of the ancient Slavs and their original significance)

524. Pilipenko, M. F. "Belorusskaia etnograficheskaia literatura o narodnykh (dokhristianskikh) verovaniiakh." in *Voprosy istorii drevnego mira i srednikh vekov.* F.M. Nechai, ed. Minsk, Izd. BGU, 1970. pp 149-64. (D53.V66) DLC CaOTU DDO ICU IEN InNd InU IU MB MH MU NcD NjP WU *USSR:* LL (Belorussian ethnographic literature about folk (pre-Christian) beliefs)

525. Pirchegger, S. "Zum altrussischen Goetternamen Stribog," *Zeitschrift fuer slavische Philologie,* 24 (1947) pp 311-6.

526. Pisani, Vittore. "Il paganesimo balto-slavo." in Tacchi Venturi, Pietro. *Storia delle religioni.* Torino, 1934-44. v. 1, pp 589-632, v. 2, pp 37-80. (BL80.T3 1939) DLC Exists in various editions. 1965 edition reviewed in *Acta Baltico-Slavica,* 6 (1969) pp 282-8.

527. Pisani, Vittore. *Le religioni dei Celti e dei Balto-Slavi, nell'Europa precristiana.* Milan, Instituto Editoriale Galileo, 1950. 103 p. (Series: Le religioni dell'umanita, 9) DDO CtY ICU MH NjP

528. Pisani, Vittore. "Simarigla, Chorsa-Dažboga." in Halle, Morris, comp. *For Roman Jakobson. Essays on the occasion of his sixtieth birthday, 11 October 1956.* The Hague, Mouton, 1956. pp 392-4. (P26.J3) DLC AAP AU CLU CoU CSt CtW CtY CU DDO FTaSU FU GAT ICN ICU IEdS InU IU KEmT KU KyU MB MCM MdBJ MH MiDW MiEM MiU MoU MtU MWelC NBC NcD NIC NN NNC NRU OClW OkU OrPS PPiU PSt PU RPB TNJ TU TxHR TxU ViU WaU WU *Great Britain:* BM

529. Pobłocki, Gustaw. "Świtowid czy Swianty Wid," *Gryf,* 2 (1910) no. 3, pp 92-4. (Swiatowit or Swianty Wid)

530. Pogodin, A. "Mythologische Spuren in russischen Dorfnamen," *Zeitschrift fuer slavische Philologie*, 11 (1934) p 35.

531. Pogodin, A. "Neskol'ko dannykh dlia russkoi mifologii v XV v," *Zhivaia starina*, 3-4 (1911) pp 425-28. (Some data for Russian mythology in the 15th century)

532. Pogodin, A. "Opyt iazycheskoi restavratsii pri Vladimire," *Trudy russkikh uchenykh zagaranitsei*, 2 (1923) pp 149-57. (An attempt at pagan restoration during Vladimir's time)

533. Polák, Vacalav. "Slovanské náboženství," *Vznik a počátky Slovanů*, 1 (1956) pp 119-32. (Slavic religion)

534. Polivka, J. "Búh Perun," *Narodnopisný sborník českoslovanský*, 2 (1898) pp 81-104. (The god Perun)

535. Pomerantseva, Erna Vasil'evna, "Iarilki," *Sovetskaia etnografiia*, 1975, no. 3, pp 127-30. (Iarilki)

536. Popov, Mikhail Vasil'evich. *Description abregee de la mythologie slavone*. St. Petersburg, 1789. *USSR*: BN

537. Popov, Mikhail Vasil'evich. *Kleine slavonische Mythologie*. St. Petersburg, J.Z. Logan, 1793. 54 p. IU

538. Popov, Mikhail Vasil'evich. "Kratkoe opisanie drevniago slavenskago iazycheskago basnosloviia." in his *Dosugi, ili sobranie sochinenii i perevodov*. St. Petersburg, Tip. Akademii nauk, 1772. v. 1, pp 186-208. (PG3317.P66D6) DLC *Great Britain*: BM *France*: BN *USSR*: BAN GPIB LL MGU SS (A brief description of ancient Slavic pagan folklore)

539. Popov, Mikhail Vasil'evich. *Kratkoe opisanie slavianskogo basnosloviia*. St. Petersburg, Tip. Sukhputnogo Shliakhetnogo Kadetskogo Korpusa, 1768. 48 p. *USSR*: LL (A brief description of Slavic folklore) See no. 540

540. Popov, Mikhail Vasil'evich. *Opisanie drevnago slavianskogo iazycheskogo basnosloviia*. St. Petersburg, 1768. 48 p. *USSR*: BAN GPIB LL SS This volume is the second edition of *Kratkoe opisanie slavianskogo basnosloviia*. (A description of ancient Slavic pagan folklore) See no. 539.

541. Porfiridov. N. G. "Zametki o dvukh arkheologicheskikh pamiatnikakh Novgorodskoog muzeia," Novgorodskii gosudarstvennyi istoricheskii muzei. *Materialy i issledovaniia*, 1 (1930) pp 31-6. (Notes on two archeological monuments of the Novgorod museum (Zbruch statue)

542. Potebnia, Aleksandr Afans'evich. "O mificheskom znachenii nekotorykh obriadov i poverii," Moscow. Universitet. Obshchestvo istorii i drevnostei rossiskikh. *Chteniia*, 53 (1865) no. 2, pp 1-84, no. 3, pp 85-232, no. 4, pp 233-310. (Concerning the mythical meaning of some beliefs and customs) See no. 381.

543. Potkanskii, K. "Wiadomości Długosza o polskiej mitologii." in his *Pisma pośmiertne.* Kraków, Nakł. Polskiej Akademji Umiejętności, 1922-24. v. 2, pp 1-93. (DK402.7P6) DLC CU ICU IU KU MH MiU NcU NNC OU PSt *Great Britain*: BM *USSR*: LL (Długosz's information about Polish mythology)

544. Potocki, Jan. *Voyage dans quelques parties de la Basse-Saxe pour la recherche des antiquités slaves ou vendes.* Hambourg, De l'Imprimerie de G.F. Schniebes, 1795. 104 p. ICN MH NB NcD NjP OCl *Great Britain*: BM *France*: BN *USSR*: LL

545. Potocki, M. & Zebrawski, T. "Wiadomości o bożyszczu słowiańskiem znaleionem w Zbruczu," Towarzystwo naukowe w Krakowe. *Rocznik*, 8 (1852) pp 3-50. (Information concerning the Slavic god found in the Zbruch river)

546. Preis, P. "Donesenie P. Preisa, G. Ministru Narodnogo Prosveshcheniia, iz Pragi, ot 26 Dekabria 1840 goda," Russia. Ministerstvo narodnogo prosveshcheniia. *Zhurnal*, 1841, ch. 29, otd. 4, pp 31-52. (A report of P. Preis to the Minister of Education, from Prague, 26 December 1840 (re Khors))

547. Privalov, Nikolai Ivanovich. *Ocherk slavianskoi mifologii.* Petrograd, T-vo Khudozh. Pechati, 1916. 19 p. *USSR*: GPIB LL (An essay on Slavic mythology)

548. Procházka, Vladimír. "Organisace kultu a kmenové zřizení polabsko-pobaltských Slovanů," *Vznik a počátky Slovanů*, 2 (1958) pp 145-68. German summary. (The cult organization and tribal system of the Polabic-Baltic Slavs)

549. Prokov'ev, V. "Religiia vostochnykh slavian," *Istoricheskii zhurnal*, 1940, no. 8, pp 72-81. (The religion of the eastern Slavs)

550. Protopopov, N. "Drevne-russkii Dazh'bog i prazdniki v chest ego," *Sem'ia i shkola*, 1873, kn. 1, no. 10, pp 412-36. (The ancient Russian god Dazhbog and the holidays in his honor)

551. Radwanski, Jan. *Krótka rzecz mitologii słowiańskiej.* Krakow, 1862. 64 p. *Great Britain*: BM (Brief points of Slavic mythology)

552. Rajewski, Zdzisław. "Co wiemy o Arkonie," *Przegląd zachodni*, 2 (1946) no. 2, pp 1046-52. (What we know about Arkona)

553. Rajewski, Zdzisław. "Pogańscy kapłani-czarodzieje w walce klasowej Słowian we wczesnym średnioweczu," *Wiadomości archeologiczne*, 39 (1975) no. 4, pp 503-9. Russian and English summaries. (Pagan priests-magicians in the class struggle of the Slavs in the early Middle Ages)

554. Rajewski, Zdzisław. "Problem Radgoszczy i Swarozyca," *Przegląd zachodni*, 4 (1948) no. 2, pp 321-5. (The problem of Radogast and Swarozit)

555. Rajewski, Zdzisław. "Zur Rolle des heidnischen Zauberer und Priestertums bei den Slawen in der Periode der Herausbildung und Festigung des Feudalsystems." in *Die Rolle der Volksmassen in der Geschichte der vorkapitalistischen Gesellschaftsformationen: zum XIV intern. Historiker-Kongress in San Francisco, 1975.* J. Herrmann & I. Sellnow, eds. Berlin, Akademie Verlag, 1975. pp 315-22. (HN19.R64) (Series: Akademie der Wissenschaften der DDR. Zentral-institut fuer alte Geschichte und Archaeologie. Veroeffentlichungen, Bd. 7) DLC CDU GU IU KU MH MiEM MoSW NIC NjP *USSR*: ANSSSR-INION GBIL GPIB LL

556. Ralston, William Ralston Shedden. *The songs of the Russian people, as illustrative of Slavonic mythology and Russian social life.* London, Ellis & Green, 1872. 447 p. Exists in various editions. (GR190.R33) DLC CLSU IaU ICN ICU MoU NcD NcU NjP OCl OrP OrPR PBm PP PPDrop PPL ViU WaS *Great Britain*: BM *USSR*: GPIB LL

557. Reiter, Norbert. "Mythologie der alten Slaven." in Haussig, Hans Wilhelm. *Woerterbuch der Mythologie.* Stuttgart, E. Klett, v. 6 (1961) pp 165-208. CtY IU MH NNC OU WU *Great Britain*: BM Reviewed in *Zeitschrift fuer Slawistik*, 13 (1968) no. 5, pp 767-71.

558. "Religiia vostochnykh slavian. Priniatie khristianstva v Drevnei Rusi." in *Tserkov v istorii Rossii (IX–1917 g.) Kriticheskie ocherki.* A.P. Kazhdan, ed. Moskva, Nauka, 1967. pp 3050. (BR932.T74) DLC CaBVaU CaOTU CLU CNoS CSt CU CU-S DDO IaAS IaU ICIU ICU IEN InU IU KU MCM MdBJ MH MiEM MiU MoSW MoU MU NIC NjP NN NNC NRU NSyU OrU OU PPiU TNJ TU ViU WaU WU *USSR*: GPIB LL (The religion of the eastern Slavs. The reception of Christianity in ancient Rus)

559. Repp, F. "Der alttschechische Goetze Zelu," *Zeitschrift fuer slavische Philologie*, 24 (1956) pp 364-8.

560. Reyman, Tadeusz. "Posąg Światowida," *Z otchłani wieków*, 8 (1933) no. 1-2, pp 1-16. (The statue of Swiatowit)

561. Richter, Johann Gottfried Ohnefalsch. *Historische Nachricht von dem Ordens-Amt Rampitz an der Oder so wohl den Goetzen-Dienst der alten Wenden*. Frankfurt on der Oder, 1740. 42 p. *Great Britain*: BM

562. Rosen-Przeworska, Janina. "Posąg tzw. Światowida i inne rzeźby kamienne z obszaru Polski." in her *Tradycje celtyckie w obrędowości protosłowian*. Wrocław, Zakład Narodowy im. Ossolińskich, 1964. pp 210-44. (GN845.P7P78) DLC CaBVaU CoU CSt CtY FTaSU InU IU MH MoU NNC WaU WU (The figure of Swiatowit and the other stone sculptures in the region of Poland)

563. Rosen-Przeworska, Janina. "Sur la genese de "Swiatowid" déité slave à quater visages," *Archeologia Polona*, 13 (1972) pp 111-45.

564. Rosen-Przeworska, Janina. "La tradition du dieu celtiques à quatre visages chez les protoslaves et slaves occidentaux," Paris. Ecole pratique des haute etudes. Centre d'etues pre et protohistoriques. *Antiquitates nationales et internationales*, 4 (1963) no. 11-16, pp 65-9.

565. Rozniecki, S. "Perun und Thor. Ein Beitrag zur Quellenkritik der russischen Mythologie," *Archiv fuer slavische Philologie*, 23 (1901) pp 462-520.

566. Rozum, Jan Vaclav. *Slovanské bájesloví*. Praha, Nákl. Rozumovym, 1857. 22 p. MH *USSR*: GPIB (Slavic folklore)

567. Rudnicki, M. "Bóstwa lechickie: Jarowit, Nyja, Świetowit, Trzgłow," *Slavia occidentalis*, 5 (1926) pp 372-419. (The gods of the western Slavs: Jarowit, Nyja, Swiatowit, Triglav)

568. Rudnicki, M. "Bóstwo lechickie: Nyja," *Slavia occidentalis*, 8 (1929) p 454. (The god of the western Slavs: Nyja)

569. Rudnyc'kyj, Jaroslav B. "Dyv-Div in Slovo o polku Ihorevi," *Studia Ucrainica*, 1 (1978) pp 75-9.

570. Rusanova, I. P. "Iazycheskoe sviatilishche na r. Gnilopiat pod Zhitomirom." in Akademiia nauk SSSR. Institut arkheologii. *Kul'tura drevnei Rusi*. A.L. Mongait, ed. Moskva, 1966, pp 233-7. (DK32.A38) DLC CaBVaU CaOTU CLU CoU CtY ICU MoU NjP NN NNC OU RPB *Great Britain*: BM *USSR*: GPIB LL (A pagan sanctuary on the Gnilopiat river below Zhitomir)

571. Russov, Stepan Vasil'evich. *Opyt o idolakh, Vladimirom v Kieve posta-vlennykh vo vremia iazychestva i sim zhe velikim kniazem unich-tozhennykh, kogda on prosvetilsia blagodatnym ucheniem khris-tianskoi very.* St. Petersburg, Grach, 1824. *Great Britain*: BM *USSR*: GPIB (About the idols which Vladimir put up in Kiev during the time of paganism, which he destroyed when he was enlightened by studying the Christian faith)

572. Růžička, Josef. *Slovanské bájesloví (mythologie).* V Olomouci, Nakl. Knih. P. Prombergera, 1907. 328 p. CtY ICU IEN InU NcU NN NNC *Great Britain*: BM *USSR*: GPIB (Slavic folklore (mythology))

573. Růžička, Josef. *Život a zvyky slovanských národů.* Praha, G. Petrů, 1924. 420 p. (BL935.S6R8 1924a) DLC CSt ICU MH MiDW NcU WU (The life and customs of the Slavic peoples)

574. Rybakov, Boris Aleksandrovich. "Drevnie elementy v russkom na-rodnom tvorcheskve," *Sovetskaia etnografiia*, 1948, no. 1, pp 90-106. (Ancient elements n Russian folk art)

575. Rybakov, Boris Aleksandrovich. "Iazycheskoe miroponimanie," *Na-uka i religiia*, 1975, no. 2, pp 56-60. (The pagan worldview)

576. Rybakov, Boris Aleksandrovich. "Iazycheskoe mirovozzrenie rus-skogo srednovekov'ia," *Voprosy istorii*, 1974, no. 1, pp 3-30. (The pagan worldview of the Russian Middle Ages)

577. Rybakov, Boris Aleksandrovich. "Iazycheskoe sviatilishche na bla-goveshchenskoie gore." in *Po sledam drevnikh kul'tur.* Moskva, Gos. Izd-vo Kul'turno-prosvetitel'noi Lit-ry, 1953. pp 108-13. (DK30.P57) DLC CaBVaU CaOTU CLU CSt CtY CU DDO ICU InU IU MH-P NBC NIC NjP NN NNC OrCS OrU OU RPB TxU WaU *USSR*: GPIB LL (The pagan sanctuary on Bla-goveshchensk mountain)

578. Rybakov, Boris Aleksandrovich. *Iazychestvo drevnikh slavian.* Moskva, Nauka, 1981. 606 p. (BL930.R9) DLC AzTeS CU-SB IU KU NcU OrU ViU WU Reviewed in *Istoriia SSSR*, 1982, no. 5, pp 186-9. (The paganism of the ancient Slavs)

579. Rybakov, Boris Aleksandrovich. "Iazychestvo i khristianstvo v Drevnei Rusi." in *Tezisy dokladov na zasedaniiakh posviashchennykh ito-gam polevykh issledovanii 1965 g.* Moskva, Inst. arkheologii ANSSSR i Inst. etnografii ANSSSR, 1966. pp 3-5. *USSR*: LL (Paganism and Christianity in Ancient Rus)

580. Rybakov, Boris Aleksandrovich. "Khristiane ili iazychniki. (Raboty sovetskikh arkheologov po izucheniiu byta i verovanii drevnikh

slavian. Interviiu)," *Nauka i religiia*, 1966, no. 2, pp 46-9. (Christians or pagans. (The words of Soviet archeologists on the study of the life and beliefs of the ancient Slavs. An interview)

581. Rybakov, Boris Aleksandrovich. "Osnovnye problemy izucheniia slavianskogo iazychestva." in International Congress of Anthropological and Ethnographical Sciences, 7th, Moscow, 1964. *Trudy*, v. 8, pp 139-44. (GN3.I39 1964) DLC CaOTU CLU CNoS CSt CtW CtY CU FMU GU ICU InU IU KU MH MH-P MiDW MiEM MiU MoSW MoU NBuU NhU NIC NjP NN NNC OrPS OrU OU PPT RPB TxU ViU WU *USSR*: LL (Fundamental problems of the study of Slavic paganism) See no. 582

582. Rybakov, Boris Aleksandrovich. *Osnovnye problemy izucheniia slavianskogo iazychestva.* Moskva, Nauka, 1964. 9 p. *USSR*: LL (Fundamental problems of the study of Slavic paganism) See no. 581

583 Rybakov, Boris Aleksandrovich. "Paganism in Mediaeval Rus," *Social Science*, 6 (1975) no. 1, pp 130-56.

584. Rybakov, Boris Aleksandrovich. "Rusalii and the god Simargl-Pereplut," *Soviet anthropology and archeology*, 6 (1968) no. 4, pp 34-59. Translation of no. 585.

585. Rybakov, Boris Aleksandrovich. "Rusali i bog Simargl-Pereplut," *Sovetskaia arkheologiia*, 1967, no. 2, pp 91-116. (Rusalii and the god Simargl-Pereplut) See no. 584

586. Rybakov, Boris Aleksandrovich. "Slavianskoie iazychestvo." in Akademiia nauk SSSR. Otdelenie istoricheskoi nauk. *Tezisy dokladov zasedaniiakh povsiashchennykh itogam polevykh issledovanii 1961 g.* Moskva, ANSSSR, 1962. pp 11-12. *USSR*: LL (Slavic paganism)

587. Rybakov, Boris Aleksandrovich. "Sviatovit-Rod." in *Liber Iosepho Kostrzewski octogenario a veneratoribus dicatus.* Wrocław, Zakład Narodowy im. Ossolińskich, 1968. pp 390-4. (CC65.L5) DLC CSt CU ICU IEN MdBWA WU *France*: BN *Great Britain*: BM

588. Rybakov, Boris Aleksandrovich. "Zadachi izucheniia slavianskogo iazycheskogo mirovozzreniia." in *Metodologicheskie voprosy obshchestvennykh nauk; sbornik statei.* D.I. Chesnokov, ed. Moskva, Izd-vo MGU, 1966. pp 369-80. (H61.M493) DLC NIC *USSR*: LL (Problems of the study of the Slavic pagan worldview)

589. Rziga, V. "Slovo o polku Igoreve i russkoe iazychestvo," *Slavia*, 12 (1933-34) pp 422-33. (The Slovo o polku Igoreve and Russian paganism)

590. S., K. J. "Bajeslovje i crkva," *Arkiv za povestnicu jugoslavensku*, 1 (1851) pp 86-104. (Folklore and the Church)

591. Sabinin, Stefan. "Volos, iazycheskoe bozhestvo slaviano-russov, sravnennoe s odnom skandinanov," Russia. Ministerstvo nardonogo prosveshcheniia. *Zhurnal*, 40 (1843) otd. 2, pp 17-52. (Volos, pagan god of the Slavo-Rus, compared with a Scandinavian (god)) See no. 592.

592. Sabinin, Stefan. "Volos, iazycheskoe bozhestvo slaviano-russov, sravnennoe s odnom skandinanov," *Zhurnal dlia chteniia vospitannikam voenno-uchebnykh zavedenii*, 47 (1844) no. 86, pop 186-99, no. 87, pp 272-95. (Volos, pagan god of the Slavo-Rus, compared with a Scandinavian (god)) See no. 591

593. Sadnik, Linda. "Ancient Slav religion in the light of recent research," *Eastern Review*, 1 (1948) no. 1, pp 36-43.

594. Sadnik, Linda. "Die Religion der Slawen." in Koenig, Franz, Cardinal. *Christus und die Religionen der Erde*. Vienna, 1951. v. 2, pp 369-79. (BL80.K6) DLC CtY-D MB MH-AH NB NcD NIC NN PU TxU WU

595. Sadnik, Linda. "Die Religion der Slawen im Altertum im Lichte der heutigen Forschung," *Blick nach Osten*, 1 (1948) no. 1, pp 38-45.

596. Šafařík, Pavel Jozef. "O statuie Chernoboga v Bambergie," *Russkii istoricheskii sbornik*, 1 (1837) kn. 1, pp 51-81. (Concerning the statue of Chernobog in Bamberg)

597. Šafařík, Pavel Jozef. "O Svaroge, bog iazycheskikh slavian," Moscow. Universitet. Obshchestvo istorii i drevnostei rossiskikh. *Chteniia*, 1 (1846) no. 1, pp 30-4. (Concerning Svarog the god of the pagan Slavs)

598. Šafařík, Pavel Jozef. "O Svarohovi, bohu pohanskych Slovanu," Prague. Národní museum. *Časopis*, 18 (1844) pp 483-89. (Concerning Svarog, the god of the pagan Slavs)

599. Šafařík, Pavel Jozef. "Podobizna Cernoboha v Bamberku," Prague. Národní museum. *Časopis*, 11 (1837) pp 23-36. (A portrait of Chernobog in Bamberg)

600. Šafařík, Pavel Jozef. *Slovanské starožitnosti.* Praha, Tiskem I. Spurného, 1837. 2v. Exists in various editions. (D147.S2) DLC CLU CSt CU InU IU MH MnU NIC TxU WaU (Slavic antiquities)

601. Šafařík, Pavel Jozef. "Swaroh, ein slawisch-heidnischer Gott," *Jahrbuecher fuer slawische Literatur, Kunst und Wissenschaft,* 3 (1845) H. 10, pp 368-71.

602. Sakharov, Ivan Petrovich. "Slaviano-russkaia mifologiia." in his *Skazaniia russkogo naroda.* St. Petersburg, 1841-49. v. 1, kn. 1, otd. 1, pp 2-22. (PG3110.S29 1841) DLC CU NN WU *Great Britain*: BM *USSR*: LL Exists in various editions. (Slavic-Russian mythology)

603. Sapunov, S. V. "Iaroslavna i drevnerusskoe iazychestvo." in Akademiia nauk SSSR. Institut russkoi literatury. *Slovo o polku Igoreve — pamiatnik XII veka.* Moskva–Leningrad, Izd-vo ANSSSR, 1962. pp 321-9. (PG3300.S6A5) DLC CLU CtY InU IU MnU NcD NIC NjP OU PPULC TxU *Great Britain*: BM *USSR*: LL (The reign of Iaroslav and ancient Russian paganism)

604. Saria, Balduin. "Ein neues altslawisches Heiligtum?," *Carinthia I,* 140 (1950) H. 1-2, pp 384-89.

605. Schaeder, Hildeg. "Die vorchristliche Religion der Nordwestslawen," *Jomsburg,* 4 (1940) pp 217-24.

606. Scheller, Friederich Johann. *Mythologie der wendischen und anderer teutschen Voelker.* Neuburg, J. J. Deininger, 1804. 202 p. NIC *Great Britain*: BM

607. Scheltz, T. "Ueber den slavischen Abgott Flyns," *Neues Lausitzisches magazin,* 20 (1842) pp 344-9.

608. Schildgen, Theodor. *St. Vitus und der slavische Swantovit i ihrer Beziehung zu einander.* Muenster, Druck der Coppenrathschen Buchdruckerei, 1881. 18 p. OCl

609. Schlimpert, G. & Witkowski, T. "Namenkundliches zum 'Rethra'-Problem," *Zeitschrift fuer Slawistik,* 14 (1969) no. 4, pp 529-44.

610. Schmaus, Alois. "Zur altslawischen Religionsgeschichte," *Saeculum,* 4 (1953) pp 206-30. See no. 611

611. Schmaus, Alois. "Zur altslawischen Relgiionsgeschichte." in his *Gesammelte slavistische und balkanologische Abhandlungen.* Munich, R. Trofenik, 1971. pp 228-59. (PG15.S33) (Series: Beitraege zur Kenntnis Suedosteuropas und des Nahen Orients, Band 14, teil

1) DLC CaBVaU CoU CSt CtY CU FTaSU FU GU InU IU KU KyU MH MiDW MiEM MiU MnU MoU NcU NIC NjP NjR NNC OCU OU TxU WaU WU See no. 610

612. Schmidt, O. "Slawische Goetterbilder in Sachsen," *Neues archiv fuer saechsische Geschichte und Altertumskunde*, 1911, pp 350-56.

613. Schmidt, Roderich. "Rethra. Das Heiligtum d. Lutizen als Heiden-Metropole." in *Festschrift fuer Walter Schlesinger*. Helmut Beumann, ed. Koeln, Boehlau, 1973-74. pp 366-94. (Series: Mittel-deutsche Forschungen, Bd. 740 (DD4.F47) DLC AzU CaBVaU CaQMM CLU CtY CU CU-S CU-SB GU IaU IU MdU MH MH-AH MiDW MiU MnU MoSW MoU MU NBuU NcD NIC NjP NN NNC NRU NSyU OClW OCU OrU PPT RPB TxU ViBlbV ViU WU

614. Schmidt, Ruediger. "Zur angeblich iranischen Herkunft des altrussi-schen Gottesnamens Stribog," *Die Welt der Slaven*, 16 (1971) no. 2, pp 193-200.

615. Schneeweis, Edmund. *Grundiss des Volksglaubens und Volksbrauchs der Serbokroaten*. Celje, Druzba sv. Mohorja, 1935. 267 p. CU ICU InU IU MH NN NNC Reviewed in *Zeitschrift fuer slavische Philologie*, 13 (1936) pp 271-74.

616. Schoeps, Hans Joachim. "Slavic religion." in his *Religions of Mankind*. Garden City, Doubleday, 1966. pp 112-6. (BL80.2S353) DLC CoU CSt CU IaU ICU IEN MH-AH NbU NjP PPULC Wau

617. Schroeder, Leopold von. "Der Himmelgott bei den Kelten, Littauern und Letten, Slaven und Phrygern." in his *Arische Religion*. Leipzig, H. Haessel, 1914. v. 1, pp 524-54. (BL660.S28) DLC CtY CU ICU MdBJ MiU NIC NN NNUT PU

618. Schubart, H. "Dei Tempelburg Arkona," *Ausgrabungen und Funde*, 3 (1958) no. 4-5, pp 305-7.

619. Schuchardt, Karl. *Arkona, Rethra, Vineta*. Berlin, H. Schoetz & Co., 1926. 101 p. (GN789.G3S35 1926) DLC CtY DDO ICU MH MiU MoU NcD WaU

620. Schuchardt, Karl. "Nochmals der Tempel in Arkona," *Zeitschrift fuer slavische Philologie*, 16 (1939) pp 152-3.

621. Schuchardt, Karl. "Rethra auf dem Schlossberge bei Feldberg im Mecklenburg," Akademie der Wissenschaften, Berlin. *Sitzungs-berichte*, 1923, pp 184-226.

622. Schuchhardt, Karl. "Rethra und Arcona," Akademie der Wissenschaften Berlin. *Sitzungsberichte*, 1921, no. 2, pp 756-74.

623. Schuetz, J. "Denkform und Sinngehalt ostslavischer Goetternamen." in Congresus Internationalis Historiae Slavicae, Salisburg-Ratisbonensis, 2d. Universitaet Salzburg, 1967. *Das heidnische und christliche Slaventum*. Wiesbaden, O. Harrassowitz, 1969-70. v. 2, pp 86-93. (PG11.C6) (Series: Institutum Salvicum Salisburgo-Ratisbonese. Annales, Bd. II, 1) For locations, see no. 180

624. Schuetz, J. "Die slavische mythologie und die Etymologie," Brussels. Université libre. Institut de philologie et d'histoire orientales et slaves. *Annuaire*, 18 (1966-67) pp 335-46.

625. Schuldt, Ewald. *Der altslawische Tempel von Gross-Raden*. Schwerin, Museum fuer Ur- und Fruehgeschichte, 1976. 63 p. (Series: Bildkatalog des Museum fuer Ur- und Fruehgeschichte Schwerin, Bd. 19) *USSR*: ANSSSR-INION BAN BANBelo BANEst

626. Schuster-Šewc, H. "Zur Frage der suedslawischen perunika-Namen," *Južnoslovenski Filolog*, 30 (1973) pp 213-21.

627. Schwartz, E. "Beitraege zur Rethrafrage," *Mannus*, 17 (1925) pp 210-7.

628. Schwenk, Konrad. *Die Mythologie der Slawen fuer Gebildete und die studierende Jugend*. Frankfurt am Main, J.D. Sauerlaender, 1853. 482 p. This is volume seven of his *Die Mythologie der asiatischen Voelker, der Aegypter, Greichen, Roemer, Germanen und Slaven*. Frankfurt am Main, J.D. Sauerlaender, 1843-53. CtY CU ICU InU IU MdBP MH NcD NIC NjP NN OCl PU ViU

629. Sedov, V. V. "Drevnerusskoe sviatilishche v Peryni," Akademiia nauk SSSR. Institut arkheologii. *Kratkie soobshcheniia o dokladakh i polevykh issledovaniiakh*, 50 (1953) pp 92-103. (The ancient Russian sanctuary in Peryn)

630. Sedov, V. V. "Iazycheskie sviatilishcha smolenskikh krivichei," Akademiia nauk SSSR. Institut arkheologii. *Kratkie soobshcheniia o dokladakh i polevykh issledovaniiakh*, 87 (1962) pp 57-64. (The pagan sanctuaries of the Smolensk Krivichi)

631. Sedov, V. V. "K voprosu o zhertvoprinosheniiakh v drevnem Novgorode," Akademiia nauk SSSR. Institut arkheologii. *Kratkie soobshcheniia o dokladakh i polevykh issledovaniiakh* 68 (1957) pp 20-30. (Concerning sacrifices in ancient Novgorod)

632. Sedov, V. V. "Novye dannye o iazycheskom sviatilishche Peruna," Akademiia nauk SSSR. Institut arkheologii. *Kratkie soobshche-*

niia o dokladakh i polevykh issledovaniiakh, 53 (1954) pp 195-208.
(New data on the pagan sanctuary of Perun)

633. Sedov, V. V. "Pagan sanctuaries and idols of the Eastern Slavs,"
Slavica Gandensia, 7-8 (1980-81) pp 69-85.

634. Sedov, V. V. "Pervyi mezhdunarodnyi simpozium po slavianskomu
iazychestvu," Akademiia nauk SSSR. Institut arkheologii. *Kratkie soobshcheniia*, 164 (1981) pp 122-5. (The first international
simposium on Slavic paganism)

635. Sesja naukowa "Religia pogańskich Słowian," Kielce, 1967. *Religia
pogańskich Słowian; sesja naukowa w Kielcach.* Alojzy Oborny,
ed. Kielce, 1968. 147 p. Summaries in English and Russian. IU
Great Britain: BM Reviewed in *Euhemer*, 13 (1969) pp 130-33.
(The religion of the pagan Slavs)

636. Shaian, Volodymyr. *Naivyshche svitlo; studiia pro Svaroga i Khorsa.*
London, Orden, 1969. 54 p. (BL935.S945S5) DLC IU OKentU
(The highest light; a study on Svarog and Khors)

637. Shelest, Walter. "Sviatovyt of Arkona and the Zbruch idol." in
Ukrains'ka vil'na akademiia nauk. *Iuvileinyi zbirnik Ukrains'koi
vil'noi akademii nauk v Kanadi.* O.V. Gerus, ed. Vinnipeg,
UVAN, 1976. pp 213-22. IU NIC

638. Shepping, Dmitrii Ottovich. *Mify slavianskogo iazychestva.* Moskva,
V tip. V Got'e, 1849. 197 p. (BL930.S53) DLC NN *USSR*: GPIB
LL Reviewed in *Otechestveniia zapiski*, 19 (1850) pp 80-6. (The
myths of Slavic paganism)

639. Shepping, Dmitrii Ottovich. "Nashi pis'mennye istochniki o iazycheskikh bogakh russkoi mifologii," *Filologicheskiia zapiski*,
1888, no. 6, pp 1-31. (Our written sources concerning the pagan
gods of Russian mythology) See no. 640

640. Shepping, Dmitrii Ottovich. *Nashi pis'mennye istochniki o iazycheskikh bogakh russkoi mifologii.* Voronezh, V tip. V.I. Isaeva, 1889.
31 p. OCl *USSR*: GPIB LL (Our written sources concerning the
pagan gods of Russian mythology) See no. 639

641. Shepping, Dmitrii Ottovich. "O mifologii russkikh slavian." in Arkhe-
ologicheskii s"ezd, 1st, Moscow, 1869. *Trudy*, v. 1, pp 249-51
NN *USSR*: LL (Concerning the mythology of the Russian Slavs)

642. Shepping, Dmitrii Ottovich. "O mifologii russkikh slavian," Moskovskoe arkheologicheskoe obshchestvo. *Drevnosti*, 1 (1871) pp
81-251. (Concerning the mythology of the Russian Slavs)

643. Shepping, Dmitrii Ottovich. *Ob istochnikakh i formakh russkago bas-nosloviia.* Moskva, 1859. 2v in 1. NN Reviewed in *Moskovskiia Viedomosti,* no. 55, (1860) pp 427-8. (Concerning the sources and forms of Russian folklore)

644. Shepping, Dmitrii Ottovich. "Opyt o znachenii Roda i Rozhanitsy," Moscow. Universitet. Obshchestvo istorii i drevnostei rossiskikh. *Vremennik,* 9 (1851) pp 25-36. (Concerning the meaning of Rod and Rozhanits)

645. Shepping, Dmitrii Ottovich. "Svietovit," Moscow. Universitet. Obshchestvo istorii i drevnostei rossiskikh. *Vremennik,* 13 (1852) pp 1-14. (Swiatowit)

646. Shepping, Dmitrii Ottovich. "Vzgliad na trudy po slavianskoi mifologii v poslednee vremia," *Moskovskiia viedomosti,* 1851, no. 91, pp 836-7. (A look at recent works on Slavic mythology)

647. Shliakov, N. V. "Troian v Slovo o polku Igoreve." in *Novyi sbornik statei po slavianovedeniiu.* V.I. Lamanskii, comp. St. Petersburg, 1905. pp 289-96 (D377.N6) DLC CaBVaU CSt CtY IU NN RPB WU *Great Britain:* BM *USSR:* LL (Troian in the Slovo o polku Igoreve)

648. Sławski, Franciszek. "Z mitologii słowiańskiej." in *Opuscula Polono-Slavica.* Jan Safarewicz, ed. Kraków, Zakład Narodowy im. Ossolińskich, 1979. pp 369-71. InU MH MiDWW MiEM NIC OU ViU WU (From Slavic mythology)

649. Smoler, Jan Ernst. "Powostanki ze starodawnego nabóżnistwa w serbskich Łužicach," Maćica Serbska, Bautzen. *Časopis,* 1 (1848) pp 217-23. (Remnants of ancient belief in Sorbian Lusatia)

650. Smoler, Jan Ernst. "Ueberreste der alten Mythologie in der wendischen Lausitz," *Zeitschrift fuer Deutsche Mythologie und Sittenkunde,* 3 (1855) pp 109-15. Translation of no. 649

651. Sobolevksii, A. I. "Volos i Vlasii," *Russkii filologicheskii vestnik,* 3 (1886) pp 185-7. (Volos and Vlasii)

652. Sokolov, Mikhail Evgen'evich. *Staro-Russkie solnechnye bogi i bogini.* Simbirsk, Tip. A. Tokareva, 1887. 179 p. (BL438.S64) DLC NN OCl OU *USSR:* GPIB LL Reviewed in Russia. Ministerstvo narodnogo prosveshcheniia. *Zhurnal,* v.254 (1887) pp 364-73. (Old Russian sun gods and goddesses)

653. Sokolowska, I. "Wczesnohistoryczne posągi kamienne odkryta na zemiach Polski," *Światowit,* 22 (1924-28) pp 116-28. (Early historical stone statues found in Poland)

654. Solov'ev, S. "Ocherk pravov, obychaei i religii slavian, preimu-shchestvennogo vostochnykh, vo vremena iazycheskiia," *Arkhiv istoriko-iuridicheskikh svedenii, otnosiashchikhsia do Rossii*, 1 (1850) pp 1-54. (An essay on the customs and religion of the Slavs, chiefly eastern, in pagan times)

655. Sommer, Eduard. "Goetzenbilder der alten Sachsen und lausitzer Sorben," *Saxonia*, 1 (1835) pp 66-7.

656. Specht, F. "Der indogermanische Himmelsgott im Baltisch-Slavi-schen," *Zeitschrift fuer vergleichende Sprachforschung auf dem Gebiete der indogermanischen Sprachen*, 1963, no. 3, pp 115-23.

657. Srebrianskii, Ivan Vasil'evich. "Mifologiia Slova o polku Igoreve (Veles, Traian-Stribog, Khors-Dazhd'bog)," Nezhin, Ukraine. Istoriko-filologicheskii institut kniazia Bezborodko. *Izvestiia*, 15 (1895) pp 3-33. (The mythology of the Slovo o polku Igoreve (Veles, Traian-Stribog, Khors-Dazhbog) See no. 658

658. Srebrianskii, Ivan Vasil'evich. *Mifologiia Slova o poku Igoreve (Veles, Traian-Stribog, Khors-Dazhd'bog)*. Nezhin, 1895. 33 p. *USSR*: LL (The mythology of the Slovo o polku Igoreve (Veles, Traian-Stribog, Khors-Dazhbog) See no. 657

659. Sreznevskii, Izmail Ivanovich. "Arkhitektura khramov iazycheskikh slavian," Moscow. Universitet. Obshchestvo istorii i drevnostei rossiskikh. *Chteniia*, 1 (1846) pp 44-54. (The architecture of the temples of the pagan Slavs)

660. Sreznevskii, Izmail Ivanovich. "Issledovaniia o iazycheskom bogo-sluzhenii drevnikh slavian," *Finskii vestnik*, 21 (1847) no. 9, otd. 2, pp 1-36, 22 (1847) no. 10, otd. 2, pp 1-20, 23 (1847) no. 11, otd. 2, pp 1-40. (Research concerning the pagan worship of the ancient Slavs) See no. 661

661. Sreznevskii, Izmail Ivanovich. *Issledovaniia o iazycheskom bogoslu-zhenii drevnikh slavian*. St. Petrsburg, Tip. K. Zhernakova, 1848. 96 p. MH NN NNC Ocl *USSR*: GPIB LL Reviewed in Russia. Ministerstvo nardonogo prosveshcheniia. *Zhurnal*, ch. 48 (1848) pp 346-64. (Research concerning the pagan worship of the ancient Slavs) See no. 660

662. Sreznevskii, Izmail Ivanovich. "Ob obozhanii solntsa u drevnikh sla-vian," Russia. Ministerstvo narodnogo prosveshcheniia. *Zhurnal*, 51 (1846) otd. 2, pp 36-60. (Concerning the adoration of the sun by the ancient Slavs) See no. 663

663. Sreznevskii, Izmail Ivanovich. *Ob obozhanii solntsa u drevnikh slavian*. St. Petersburg, 1846. 25 p. *USSR*: LL (Concerning the adoration of the sun by the ancient Slavs) See no. 662

664. Sreznevskii, Izmail Ivanovich. "Rozhenitsy u slavian i drugikh iazy-cheskikh narodov," *Arkhiv istoriko-iuridicheskikh svedenii, otno-siashchikhsia do Rossii*, 1855, kn. 2, otd. 1, pp 97-122. (Birth among the Slavs and other pagan peoples) See no. 665

665. Sreznevskii, Izmail Ivanovich. *Rozhenitsy u slavian i drugikh iazyches-kikh narodov*. Moskva, Tip. Aleksandra Semena, 1855. 26 p. DLC *Great Britain*: BM *USSR*: LL (Birth among the Slavs and other pagan peoples) See no. 664

666. Sreznevskii, Izmail Ivanovich. *Sviatilishcha i obriady iazycheskogo bogosluzheniia drevnikh slavian*. Khar'kov, V Univ. tip., 1846. 107 p. IU NPV WU *USSR*: GPIB LL (The sanctuaries and customs of the pagan worship of the ancient Slavs)

667. Sreznevskii, Izmail Ivanovich. "Ueber den Sonnerdienst der alten Slaven," *Archiv fuer wissenschaftliche Kunde von Russland*, 6 (1848) pp 76-90.

668. Sreznevskii, Izmail Ivanovich. "Zbruchskii istukan Krakovskogo muzeia," Moskovskoe arkheologicheskoe obshchestvo. *Zapiski*, 5 (1853) vyp. 2-3, pp 163-96. (The Zbruch idol of the Krakow museum)

669. Steinbrueck, J. J. *Vom Goezzendienst in Pommern und Ruegen*. Stettin, Gedruch mit leichschen Schristen, 1792. 44 p. *Great Britain*: BM *USSR*: GPIB

670. Stender-Petersen, A. "Russian paganism," *Acta Jutlandica*, 28 (1956) pp 44-53.

671. Stichtenoth, D. "Farria vel Heiligland und das Ruegenheiligtum. Eine Entgegnung," Gesellschaft fuer schleswig-holsteinische Geschich-te, Kiel. *Zeitschrift*, 77 (1953) pp 184-95.

672. Strekelj, K. "Helmold's Zcerneboch im angelsaechischen Olymp," *Archiv fuer slavische Philologie*, 26 (1904) p 320.

673. Stroev, Pavel Mikhailovich. *Kratkoe obozrenie mifologii slavian ros-siskikh*. Moskva, Tip. S. Selivanskogo, 1815. 43 p. (BL930.S68) DLC NN *Great Britain*: BM *USSR*: GPIB (A brief review of the mythology of the Russian Slavs)

674. Struve, Karl W. "Eine Steinstatuette aus Ratzeburg als Beitrag zur slawischen Religionsgeschichte," Heimatbund und Geschichts-verein Herzogtum Lauenburg. *Schriftreihe*, 21 (1958) pp 1-11.

675. Stuhlmann, C. W. "Die wendischen Schwerine. Ein Beitrage zur Erlaeuterung des slavischen Goetzendienstes," *Globus*, 15 (1869) pp 1-11.

676. Sucić, Nikola. *Hrvatska narodna mitologija.* Zagreb, Grafika, 1943. 198 p. (Series: Psihologija i psihopatologija čovječanstva, dio 2) CaBVaU InU (Croatian folk mythology)

677. "Światowid w Arkonie," *Przyjaciel ludzi,* 1836, no. 7, pp 47-8. (Swiatowit in Arkona)

678. Świerzbienski, K. "Rok, bóstwo Słowianie, jego kapłani i obrzędy," *Dwutygodnik naukowy,* 1879, pp 481-6, 500-511. (Rok, god of the Slavs, his priests and rites)

679. Świerzbinski, R. *Wiara Słowian.* Warszawa, Nakł. autora, 1880. 2nd ed. 1884. IU (The beliefs of the Slavs)

680. Syrka, P. "Slaviansko-rumynskie otryvki, I. Rumynskii sfarog i slavianskii Svarog," Russia. Ministerstvo narodnogo prosveshcheniia. *Zhurnal,* 52 (1887) otd. 2, pp 1-17. (Slavic-Rumanian fragments. I. Rumanian Sfarog and Slavic Svarog)

681. Sz., W. "Czy Schuchhardt odkrył świątynie Świętowita?" *Z otchłani wieków,* 25 (1959) no. 6, pp 415-6. (Did Schuchhardt find Swiatowit's temple?)

682. Szafrański, Włodzimierz. "Nowa rewelacja archeologiczna (jeszcze o Płockim wczesnośredniowieczym uroczysku pogańskim)," *Notatki Płockie,* 1974, no. 4, pp 44-9, no. 5, pp 14-8. (A new archeological discovery (More about the Płock early medieval pagan sacred spot)

683. Szafrański, Włodzimierz. "O periodyzacje pradziejów wierzeń słowiańskich. Zur Periodisierung der Urgeschichte der slawischen heidnischen Religionen." in *Congres international d'archeologie slave,* 1st, Warsaw, 1965. Wrocław, Zakład Narodowy im. Ossolińskich, v. 2 (1968) pp 379-85. Texts in Polish and German. For locations, see no. 114

684. Szafrański, Włodzimierz. "Religia Słowian." in *Zarys dziejów religii.* Zygmunt Poniatowski, ed. Warszawa, 1964. pp 477-91. Exists in various editions. (Slavic religion)

685. Szafrański, Włodzimierz. "Ślady kultu bożka Welesa u plemion wczesno-polskich," *Archeologia Polski,* 3 (1959) no. 1, pp 159-65. Russian summary. (Traces of the god Veles' cult among the early Polish tribes)

68. Szafrański, Włodzimierz. "Un lieu du culte païen du haut moyen age decouvert a Płock," *Archeologia Polona,* 3 (1960) pp 167-71.

687. Szulc, Kazimierz. *Mythyczna historya Polska i mythologia Słowiańska.* Poznan, 1880. 243 p. MH *Great Britain*: BM Reviewed in *Biblio-*

teka warszawska, 1882, no. 1, pp 122-36. (The mythological history of Poland and Slavic mythology)

688. Szulc, Kazimierz. *O głównych wyobrażeniach i uroczystościah bałwochwalczych naszego ludu. Z powodu prac J. Lelewela: "Bałwochwalstwo Słowian" i R. Berwińskiego: "Studia nad literatura ludowa".* Poznan, 1857. 64 p. *Great Britain*: BM *France*: BN (Concerning the chief ideas and idolatrous ceremonies of our people. From the works of J. Lelewel: *Slavic paganism* and R. Berwinski: *A study of folk literature*) See no. 399

689. Szyc, Joachim. *Słowianscy bogowie.* Warszawa, 1865. 54 p. *Great Britain*: BM (Slavic gods)

690. Szyc, Joachim. "Słowiańskie bogowie," *Przeglad tygodniowy*, 1866, pp 93-4. (Slavic gods)

691. Teige, J. "Die Gottheit Zelu," *Archiv fuer slavische Philologie*, 7 (1884) pp 645-6.

692. Telegin, D. IA. "Dvogolove staroslov'ians'ke bozhestvo," *Pam'iatnyky Ukrainy*, 1972, no. 3, p 46. (The two-headed old Slavic god)

693. Thomas, Heinz. *Die slawische und baltische Religion vergleichend darstellt.* Wohlau, 1934. 83 p. CtY ICRL NjP PU *France*: BN

694. Thunmann, Hans Erich. "Ueber die gottesdienstlichen Alterhuemer der Obotriten." in Masch, Andreas gottlieb. *Beytraege zur Erlaeuterung der obotritischen Altrthuemer.* Schwerin und Guestrow bei Buchenroeder und Ritter, 1774. pp 3-58. *Great Britain*: BM *USSR*: LL

695. Thunmann, Hans Erich. "Ueber die gottesdienstlichen Alterthuemer der Obotriten." in his *Untersuchungen ueber die alte Geschichte einiger nordischen Voelker.* Berlin, 1772. pp 294-323. ICN MB NIC

696. Tielemann, Gotthard Tobias. "Perkun der Donnergott der alten Slaven." in his *Livona. Ein historisch-poetisches Taschenbuch fuer die deutsch-russischen Ostsee Provinzen.* Riga, F. Meinhausen, v. 2 (1815) pp 145-56. ICU MH NN PPLT *Great Britain*: BM

697. Tikhomirov, M. N. "Iazycheskoe mirovozzrenie i khristianstvo." in *Religiia i tserkov' v istorii Rossii: sovetskie istoriki o pravoslavnoi tserkvi v Rossii.* A.M. Saharova, ed. Moskva, Mysl', 1975. pp 42-6. (BX485.R35) DLC CaBVaU CaOTU CSt-H CU CU-SB ICU InU IU KU MB MH MiU MnU MU NcU NjP NNC TNJ ViU WaU WU *USSR*: GPIB LL (The pagan world view and Christianity)

698. Tikhonravov, N. K. "Slova i poucheniia napravlennye protiv iazy-cheskikh verovanii i obriadov." in *Lietopisi russkoi literatury i drevnosti*. Moskva, V tipografii Gracheva i Ko, v. 4 (1862) otd. 2, pp 83-112. (PG2900.L5) DLC CtY NN OrU *USSR*: LL (Speeches and sermons directed against pagan beliefs and ceremonies)

699. Tille, Vaclav. "O púvodu náboženstvi starých Slovanů," Českoslo-venská akademie věd. *Vestník*, 36 (1927) pp 39-44. (Concerning the origin of the mythology of the ancient Slavs)

700. Timoshchuk, B. A. & Rusanova, I. P. "Slavianskie sviatilishcha na srednem Dnestre i v basseine Pruta: (arkheol. dannye)," *Sovet-skaia arkheologiia*, 1983, no. 4, pp 161-73. English summary. (Slavic sanctuaries on the middle Dnestr and in the basin of the Prut: archeological data)

701. Tkány, Anton. *Mythologie der alten Teutschen und Slaven*. Znaim, Gedruckt bei M. Hofmann, 1827. 2v in 1. (BL850.T5) DLC CLU CtY ICU InU IU MB MH

702. Tobolka, Z. V. "Bog Veles," *Bŭlgarska sbirka*, 8 (1901) no. 8, pp 533-7. (The god Veles)

703. Tobolka, Z. V. "O Veselovi," *Český lid*, 3 (1894) pp 529-33. (Con-cerning Veles)

704. Tokarev, Sergei Aleksandrovich. "Die altslawische Religion." in his *Die Religion in der Geschichte der Voelker*. Berlin, Dietz Verlag, 1968. pp 258-74. (BL80.2T615) DLC InU MiDW NjPT OU WU

705. Tokarev, Sergei Aleksandrovich. "Niederle's views on the religious beliefs of the ancient Slavs in the light of the latest research," *Ethnologia slavica*, 1 (1969) pp 47-66. Russian summary.

706. Tokarev, Sergei Aleksandrovich. "Religiia drevnikh slavian." in his *Religiia v istorii narodov mira*. Moskva, Nauka, 1964. pp 179-91. Also 1965 edition. (BL80.2T6) DLC IU MiU NNC NSyU OU *USSR*: GPIB LL (The religion of the ancient Slavs)

707. Tokarev, Sergei Aleksandrovich. *Religioznye verovaniia vostochno-slavianskikh narodov XIX–nachala XX veka*. Moskva–Leningrad, Izd-vo ANSSSR, 1957. 163 p. (BL930.T6) DLC CLU CU ICU InU MH NIC NjP NNC RPB WU *USSR*: GPIB LL Reviewed in *Anthropos*, 53 (1958) no. 1-2, pp 652-5. (The religious beliefs of the eastern Slavic peoples from the nineteenth to the begin-ning of the twentieth century)

708. Tomicka, Joanna. *Drzewo życia: ludowa wizja świata i człowieka.* Warszawa, Ludowa Spółdzielnia Wydawnicza, 1975. 225 p. (BD516.T65) DLC CLU CSt CU ICU InU IU MH MiU MU NcD N WaU WU *USSR*: ANSSSR-INION BLitSSR GBIL LErm (The tree of life: the folk view of the world and man)

709. Tomicki, Ryszard. "Żmij, Żmigrody, Wały Żmijowe, z problematyki religii predchrześcijańskich Słowian," *Archeologia Polski,* 19 (1974) no. 2, pp 483-508. English summary. (Zmij, Zmigrody, Waly Zmijowe, from the problems of the religion of the pre-Christian Slavs)

710. Toporov, V. N. "Fragment slavianskoi mifologii." Akademiia nauk SSSR. Institut slavianovedeniia. *Kratkie soobshcheniia,* 30 (1961) pp 14-32. (A fragment of Slavic mythology)

711. Trębaczkiewicz-Oziemska, Teresa. "Rola kapłanów pogańskich w życiu plemion polabskich." in *Na granicach archeologii.* A. Nadolski, ed. Łódz, 1968. pp 137-43. English summary. (CC165. N2) DLC IU MH (Series: Acta archeologica lodziensia, no. 17) (The role of the pagan priests in the life of the Polabian tribes)

712. Tret'iakov, P. N. "Gorodishcha-sviatilishcha levoberezhnoi smolenshchiny," *Sovetskaia arkheologiia,* 1958, no. 4, pp 170-86. (The ancient town site-sanctuaries on the left bank of the Smolenshchina)

713. Trstenjak, Davorin. "Raziskavanja na polji staroslovanske mythologie," Matica slovenská, *Letopis,* 1869, pp 1-24, 1870, pp 3-25, 1871, pp 172-92. (Research in the field of Slavic mythology)

714. Trstenjak, Davorin. *Triglav, mythologično raziskavanje.* Ljubljana, 1870. 24 p. (Triglav, a mythological investigation)

715. Truc, Gonzague. "Les Slaves." in his *Histoire des Religions.* Paris, Spes, 1962. pp 165-68. CU ICU IEG MH NN WU

716. Tyszkiewicz, J. "O schyłkowym pogaństwie na ziemiach polskich," *Kwartalnik historyczny,* 1966, no. 3, pp 549-62. Russian and French summaries. (Concerning the decline of paganism on Polish lands)

717. "Ueber die Bedeutung der altslavische Goetzenbilder, welche Wladimir in Kiew aufstellte," *Archiv fuer wissenschaftliche Kunde von Russland,* 11 (1851) pp 279-91.

718. Unbegaun, B. Q. "L'Ancienne religion les Slaves de la Baltique," *Revue d'histoire et de philosophie religieuses,* 26 (1946) pp 211-34.

719. Unbegaun, B. Q. "La religion des anciens slaves." in *Mana; introduction a l'histoire des religions.* Paris, Presses Universitaires de France, 1948. v. 2, pp 389-445. (BL80.M185) DLC CU ICU NIC NN OCl

720. Unger, E. "Rethra. Das Heiligtum der Wenden in Mecklenburg," *Offa*, 2 (1952) pp 101-12.

721. Unger, E. "Rethra-Wanzka, das seit 575 Jahre gesuchte slawische Heiligtum im Spiegel von Sagen und Flurnamen," *Forschungsfragen unserer Zeit*, 5 (1958) pp 39-53.

722. Urbańczyk, Stanisław. "Die mythologischen Arbeiten (A. Brueckner)," *Zeitschrift fuer Slawistik*, 25 (1980) no. 2, pp 216-226.

723. Urbańczyk, Stanisław. "O rekonstrucję religii pogańskich Słowian." in *Religia pogańskich Słowian; sesja naukowa w Kielcach.* Kielce, 1968. pp 29-46. (Concerning the reconstruction of the religion of the pagan Slavs) See no. 635.

724. Urbańczyk, Stanisław. *Religia pagańskich Słowian.* Krakow, 1947. 89 p. (Series: Krakow. Uniwersytet Jagellionski. Studium Słowiańskie. Biblioteka. Seria B, no. 6) CtY CU InU MH MiU PU *France*: BN *USSR*: LL MGU Reviewed in *Slavia*, 20 (1950-51) pp 483-5. (The religion of the pagan Slavs)

725. Urbańczyk, Stanisław. "Wierzenia plemion prapolskich." in Poznanskie Towarzystwo przyjaciol nauk. *Poczatki państwa Polskiego; ksiega tysiaclecia.* K. Tymieniecky, ed. Poznań, 1962. v. 2, pp 137-53. (DK421.2P68) DLC IU MH *Great Britain*: BM *France*: BN *USSR*: LL MGU (The beliefs of the early Polish tribes)

726. Urbańczyk, Stanisław. "Ze studiów nad dawną religia Słowian (komentarz do "Kroniki Czeskiej" Kosmasa, Ks III, r. 1)," *Slavia antiqua*, 27 (1980) pp 191-5. French summary. (From studies on the early religion of the Slavs. A commentary on the Czech chronicle of Cosmas, Book III, section 1)

727. Ursinus, "Von einem vermeintlichen sorbishcne Goezenbildgen in der meissnischen Gegend," *Magazin der saechischen Geschichte*, 3 (1786) pp 216-21.

728. Ushkov, S. I. "Nachertanie slavianskoi mifologii." in Lionnois, Jean Joseph. *Traité de la mythologie à l'usage des jeunes gens de l'un et de l'autre sexe.* St. Petrsburg, V. morskoi tip., 1815. Part 4. (BL305.L5 1815) DLC NN (An outline of Slavic mythology)

729. Uspenskii, Boris Andreevich. *Filologicheskie razyskaniia v oblasti sla-vianskikh drevnostei.* Moskva, Izd-vo Moskovskogo Universiteta, 1982. 246 p. AzTeS AzU CU-SB DDO InLP InU IU MiEM OU PPiU TxU WaU (Philological research in the field of Slavic antiquities)

730. Uspenskii, Boris Andreevich. "Iazycheskie refleksy v slavianskoi khristianskoi terminologii," *Slavica gandensia,* 6 (1979) pp 23-7. (Pagan reflections in Slavic Christian terminology)

731. Vaillant, Andre. "Le dieu slave Rojan," *Prilozi za književnost, istoriju, jezik i folklor,* 22 (1956) no. 3-4, pp 188-92.

732. Vasiljev, S. *Slovenska mitologija.* Srbobran, Stamparija Jevte Radaka, 1928. 94 p. IU (Slavic mythology)

733. Vei, Mrk. "K etimologii drevnerusskogo Stribog," *Voprosy iazyko-znaniia,* 7 (1958) no. 3, pp 96-9. (The etymology of the ancient Russian Stribog)

734. Velkov, Ivan. "Slaviansko svetilishte do Glava Panega," Bulgarska akademiia na naukite, Sofia. Arkheologicheski institut. *Izvestiia,* 18 (1952) pp 378-84. (The Slavic sanctuary at Glava Panega)

735. Vernadksy, George. "Svantevit, dieu les slaves Baltiques," Brussels. Université libre. Institut de philologie et d'historie orientales et slavs. *Annuaire,* 7 (1939-44) pp 339-56.

736. Vil'chinskii, Ol'gerd Frantsevich. *Kapishcha i kumiry u slavian.* St. Petersburg, Tip. V.D. Smirnova, 1904. 16 p. *USSR:* GPIB LL (Temples and idols among the Slavs)

737. Vilinbakhov, V. B. "Baltiisko-slavianskii Ruian v otrazhenii russkogo fol'klora," *Russkii fol'klor,* 11 (1968) pp 177-84. (Balto-Slavic Ruegen in the reflection of Russian folklore)

738. Vilinbakhov, V. B. "Baltiisko-slavianskii Sviatovit v fol'klore vos-tochnykh slavian." in *Ateizm, Religiia, Sovremennost'.* V.N. Sherdakov, ed. Leningrad, Nauka, 1973, vyp. 1, pp 190-8. (BL2775.2A78 1973) DLC CaOTU CtY CU-SB DS IEN InU IU MH MoU MU NcU NjP OrU PPiU WU *USSR:* LL (Balto-Slavic Swiatowit in the folklore of the eastern Slavs)

739. Vilinbakhov, V. B. "Taina ostrova Buiana (po sledam ischeznovshei tsivilizatsii slavian iazychnikov XI–XII vv na o. Rugen v Balt. more)," *Nauka i religiia,* 1967, no. 9, pp 52-5. (The secret of the island of Buian (based on the remains of the vanished civilization of the pagan Slavs of the XI–XII centuries on the island of Rue-gen in the Baltic)

740. Vinokur, I. S. & Khotiun, G. N. "Iazycheskie izvaianiia iz s. Stavchany v Podnestrov'e," *Sovetskaia arkheologiia*, 1964, no. 4, pp 210-4. (Pagan sculptures from the village of Stavchana in the lower Dnestr region)

741. Vinokur, I. S. "Iazycheskie izvaianiia na territorii Srednego Podnestrov'ia." in *Tezy dopovidei Podil'skoi istoriko-kraeznauchnoi konferentsii (zhovten' 1965 g.).* Kamenents-Podol'skii, 1965. pp 77-9. *USSR*: LL (Pagan sculptures on the territory of the middle Dnestr region)

742. Vinokur, I. S. "Iazycheskie izvaianiia Srednego Podnestrov'ia." in *Istoriia i arkheologiia iugo-zapadnykh oblastei SSSR nachala nashei ery.* B.A. Rybakov & E.A. Symonovich, eds. Moskva, Nauka, 1967. pp 136-43. (GN824.V618) DLC CLU CSt CU DDO IaU MH MiU MU NcU NIC NSyU OrU RPB ViU *USSR*: GPIB LL (Pagan sculptures of the middle Dnestr region)

743. Vinokur, I. S. "Novye iazycheskie pamiatniki na srednem Dnestre." in *Drevnie Slaviane i ikh sosedi.* IU. V. Kukharenko, ed. Moskva, Nauka, 1970. pp 38-40. (Series: Materialy i issledovaniia po arkheologii SSSR, no. 176) (DK30.M3 no. 176) DLC CaBVaU CaOTU CLSU CLU CSt DDO IaU IU KyU MiU NIC NNC OrU PSt RPB TxU WU *USSR*: TPIB LL (New pagan relics on the middle Dnestr)

744. Vinokur, I. S. "Novye nakhodki iazycheskikh izvaianii v Srednem Podnestrov'e." in *Congres international d'archeologie slave,* 1st, Warsaw, 1965. Wrocław, Zakład Narodowy im. Ossolińskich, v. 5 (1970) pp 378-88. English summary. For locations, see no. 114 (New discoveries of pagan sculptures in the middle Dnestr region)

745. Virchow, R. "Ueber die sogenannten Idole von Prillwitz und das Werk von Kollar," *Zeitschrift fuer Ethnologie,* 10 (1878) pp 264-8.

746. Vladimirov, P. V. "Poucheniia protiv drevnerusskogo iazychestva." in *Pamiatniki drevne-russkoi tserkovno-uchitel'noi literatury.* St. Petersburg, v. 3 (1897) pp 195-223. IU MH *USSR*: LL Available from Inter Documentation Company. (Sermons against ancient Russian paganism)

747. Vocel, Jan Erazim. "O bohu Velesu," Prague. Národní museum. *Časopis,* 1875, pp 405-16. (Concerning the god Veles)

748. Volkov, G. "Nechto o Velese," *Vestnik Evropy,* 1819, ch. 107, o. 19, pp 174-83. (Something about Veles) See no. 788

749. Voracek, J. A. "Perunova slavnost v Rhodopách," *Slovanský sborník*, 5 (1886) pp 26-31, 77-81, 123-6. (Perun celebration in Rhodopach)

750. Voráček, J. A. "Pohanské oběti u Bulharů. Příspevek k slovanské mythologii," *Slovanský sobrník*, 2 (1883) pp 507-13, 533-40. (Pagan sacrifices among the Bulgarians. A contribution to Slavic mythology)

751. Vulcanescu, Romulus. "Des éléments slaves dans la mythologie roumaine," *Československá etnografie*, 10 (1962) pp 178-97.

752. Vulpius, Christian August. *Handwoerterbuch der Mythologie der deutschen, verwandten, benachbarten in nordischen Voelker.* Leipzig, Lauffer, 1826. 352 p. CLU *Great Britain*: BM *France*: BN

753. Vyncke, Frans. *De godsdienst der Slaven.* Rome, Roermond, 1969 (1970). 204 p. (BL930.V93) DLC IU MH-AH NIC NN

754. Vyncke, Frans. "Het slavisch heidendom. Resultaten en mogelijkheden van het onderzoek." in Nederlands Filologen-Congres, 24th , 1956. *Handelingen*, pp 72-7.

755. Vyncke, Frans. "Methode comparative et postulats methodiques dans l'etude de la religion des anciens Slaves." in International Congress of Slavists, 5th, Sofia. *Communications présentées par les Slavisants de Belgique au Vène Congrès International de Slavistique a Sofia.* Brussels, 1963. pp 29-46. NcU

756. Vyncke, Frans. "La Religion des Slaves." in *Historie des Religions.* H.C. Puech, ed. Paris, 1970. pp 695-719. (Series: Encyclopédie de la Pléiade, 29) (BL80.2H53) DLC CaOTU CLU CSt CtY IaU IEN InU KyU LU MiDW MiEM MiU MU NBuU NcD NcU NjP NRU OkU OU PPiU RPB TU TxU WaU

757. Vyncke, Frans. "The Religion of the Slavs." in Bleeker, Claas J. *Historia Religionum.* Leiden, E. J. Brill, 1969-71. v. 1, pp 649-66. (BL80.2B55) DLC AAP AU CaBVaU CLSU CLU CNoS CoFS CoU CtW CtY CtY-D CU CU-S CU-SB CU-SC FTaSU FU GU IaAS IaU ICU IEG IEN InNd InU KyU LU MdU MH MH-AH MiEM MiU MnU MoSW MtU MU MWelC NBC NbU NBuU NcD NCRS NcU NIC NjP NjPT NjR NN NC NSyU OkU OrU PPiU PSt RPB ScU TU TxHR UU ViU VtMiM VtU WaU WU

758. Vyncke, Frans. "Trojan," Belgrad. Univerzitet. Filoloski fakultet. *Anali*, 4 (1964) pp 437-42. (Troian)

759. Wackenroder, Ernst Heinrich. *Altes und Neues Ruegen.* Grieffswald und Stralsund, 1732. *Great Britain*: BN

761. Wasilewski, T. "O śladach kultu pogańskiego w toponomastyce sło-wiańskiej Istrii," *Onomastica*, 6 (1958) pp 149-52. (Concerning the remains of a pagan cult in the toponymy of Slavic Istria)

762. Wawrzeniecki, Marjan. "Znamiona orjentalne w kamiennym słupie t.zw. Światowita," *Wiadomości archeologiczne*, 10 (1929) pp 154-7. (Oriental characteristics in the stone column, the so called Swiatowit)

763. Weber, Leo. "Nachtraeglisches zu Svantevit," *Archiv fuer Relgions-wissenschaft*, 29 (1931) pp 207-8.

764. Weber, Leo. "Svantevit und sein Heiligtum," *Archiv fuer Religions-wissenschaft*, 29 (1931) pp 70-8.

765. Weber, Leo. "Zur Eleusis und Arkona." *Archiv fuer Religionswissen-schaft*, 31 (1934) pp 170-5.

766. Weigel, M. "Bildwerke aus altslavischer Zeit," *Archiv fuer Anthropo-logie*, 21 (1892-93) pp 41-72.

767. Wendt, Karl. "Das Wendenheiligutm Rethra und die Geschichte seiner Erforschug." in his *Geschichte der Worderstadt Neubran-denburg in Einzeldarstellungen.* Neubrandenburg, Moerke, 1922. pp 248-51. MH

768. Wicaz, Ota. "Podobizna Čornoboha w Babinje," *Lužica*, 41 (1926) pp 4-6. (A portrait of Chernobog in Bamberg)

769. Wicaz, Ota. "Podobizny serbskich přibohow," *Lužica*, 41 (1926) pp 31- (Portraits of the Sorbic gods)

770. Wienecke, Erwin. "Czorneboh und Bieloboh. Eine quellenkritische Studie aus der slawischen Religionsgeschichte," *Bautzener Ge-schichtshefte*, 4 (1927) H. 6, pp 205-40.

771. Wienecke, Erwin. *Untersuchungen zur Religion der Westslaven.* Leip-zig, O. Harrassowitz, 1940. 327 p. (Series: Forschugen zur Vor- und Fruehgeschichte, 1. Heft) (BL930.W5) DLC CtY RPB *Great Britain*: BM *France*: BN Reviewed in *Slavia occidentalis*, 18 (1939-47) pp 459-70.

772. Wiesołowski, Krzysztof. "O starożytnościach religiynych Sławian pierwszych mieszkańców Polski," Towarzystwo warszawskie przyjaciol nauk. *Rocznik*, 9 (1816) pp 280-95. (Concerning the religious antiquities of the first Slavs in Poland)

773. Witkowski, Teodolius. "Mythologische Motivierte altpolabische Orts-namen," *Zeitschrift fuer Slawistik*, 15 (1970) no. 3, pp 368-85.

774. Witkowski, Teodolius. "Der Name der Redarier und ihres zentralen Heiligtums," *Zeitschrift fuer Slawistik*, 13 (1968) no. 5, pp 405-15. See no. 775

775. Witkowski, Teodolius. "Der Name der Redarier und ihres zentralen Heiligtums," in *Symbolae philologicae in honorem Vitoldi Taszycki*. S. Hrabec, ed. Wrocław, Zakład Narodowy im. Ossolińskich, 1968. pp 405-15. (Series: Polska Akademia nauk, Prace komisji językoznawstwa, no. 17) (PG14.T3) DLC CaBVaU CLU CSt CtY CU ICU InU IU MiU NcU NIC NjP NN OkU OU ViU *Great Britain*: BM See no. 774

776. Witkowski, Teodolius. "Perun" und "Mokoš" in altpolabischen Ortsnamen," *Onomastica*, 16 (1971) pp 178-84.

777. Wittoch, Z. "L'Image de la culture chrétienne et de la mythologie des slaves, conservée dans le lexique de la langue roumaine." in Congressus Internationalis Historiae Slavicae, Salisburgo-Ratisbonensis, 2d, Universitaet Slazburg, 1967. *Das heidnische und christliche Slaventum*. Wiesbaden, O. Harrassowtiz, 1969-70. v. 2, pp 158-64. (PG11.C6) (Series: Institutum Slavicum Salisburgo-Ratisbonese. Annales, Bd. II, 1) For locations, see no. 180

778. Wolter, E. "Goettersteine und Steinbilder in Sudrussland, Boehmen und Litauen," *Archiv fuer Religionswissenschaft*, 2 (1899) pp 258-61.

779. Worbs, "Sollte wirklich die Sage von einem wendischen Abgott Flins historischen Grund haben?" *Neues Lausitzisches Magazin*, 1 (1822) pp 572-

780. Wossidlo, R. "Altheilige Staetten in Mecklenburg," *Zeitschrift des Heimatbundes Mecklenburg*, 14 (1919) pp 41-54.

781. Wuerkert, Ludwig. *Mythologie der Griechen, Roemer, Zegypter, Nordlaender, Wenden und Slaven*. Leipzig, Wigand, 1838. 230 p. PU

782. Zaborowski, S. "Origines de la mythologie ancienne des slaves," *Revue anthropologique*, 17 (1907) pp 269-82.

783. Zakharov, Alexis A. "The statue of Zbrucz," *Eurasia septentrionalis antiqua*, 9 (1934) pp 336-48.

784. Żaki, A. "Stulecie odkrycia posągu tak zwanego Światowida," *Z otchłani wieków*, 17 (1948) no. 9-10, pp 129-31. (The centennial of the discovery of the so called Swiatowit)

785. Zalizniak, A. A. "Slaviano-iranskie skozhdeniia v mifologicheskoi i religiozno-etnicheskoi oblasti." pp 41-44 of his "Problemy sla-

viano-iranskikh iazykovykh otnoshenii drevneishego perioda," *Voprosy slavianskogo iazykoznaniia*, 1962, no. 6, pp 28-45. (Slavo-Iranian similarities in the mythological and ethno-religious fields)

786. Zalozetskii, Vasilii Dmitrievich. *Dazhd'bog Khors, Lada Mokosh, Svetovit.* L'vov, Prikarpatskaia Rus', 1911. 56 p. USSR: GPIB (Dazhbog Khors, Lada Mokosh, Swiatowit)

787. Zamaleev, A. "Khristianstvo i iazychestvo v Kievskoi Rusi," *Nauka i religiia*, 1972, no. 5, pp 59-63. (Christianity and paganism in Kievan Rus)

788. "Zamechaniia na stat'iu "Nechto o Velese," *Vestnik* Evropy, 1819, ch. 108, no. 21, pp 34-48. (Remarks on the article "Something on Veles) See no. 748

789. Zawilinski, R. "Ein Beitrag zur slavischen Mythologie," *Archiv fuer slavische Philologie*, 11 (1888) p 160.

790. Zečević, Slobodan. "Juznoslovenski mitski folklor u ocima stranaca i Slovena," Narodno stvaralaštvo. *Folklor*, 2 (1963) pp 602-9. (Yugoslav mythological folklore in the eyes of foreigners and Slavs)

791. Zguta, Russell. "The pagan priests of early Russia: some new insights," *Slavic Reveiw*, 33 (1974) no. 2, pp 259-66.

792. Zíbrt, C. "Neco o bohu Veselu," *Slovanský sborník*, 5 (1886) pp 318-9. (Something about the god Veles)

793. Zíbrt, C. "Vybajene pokusy o vklad bozstva Triglava," *Český lid*, 17 (1910) pp 44-5. (An attempt at an interpretation of the god Triglav)

794. Žic, N. "O Perunovu kultu u Istri," *Historijski zbornik*, 6 (1954) no. 1-4, pp 233-4. (Concerning Perun's cult in Istria)

795. Zimmermann, "Noch einige Worte ueber die Echtheit der obotriti-schen Alterthuemer, insbesondere der alten wendischen Goetzen," *Freimuethiges Abenblatt*, 10 (1828) no. 941, pp 449-52.

796. Živančević, V. "Volos," "Veles" slavianskoe bozhestvo teriomorfnogo proiskhozhdeniia." in International Congress of Anthropological and Ethnographical Sciences, 7th, Moscow, 1964. *Trudy*, v. 8, pp 46-9. (GN3.I39 1964) For locations see no. 581 (Volos-Veles, a Slavic god of earthly origin)

797. Znayenko, Myroslava T. *The gods of the anicent Slavs. Tatishchev and the beginnings of Slavic mythology.* Columbus, Slavica, 1980.

221 p. DLC AU AzTeS AzU CoU InU KyU OKentU OkU OOxM OU PPiU PPT ViBlbV WaU Wu

798. Znayenko, Myroslava T. "The mythological interests of Kievan scholars in the seventeenth and beginning of the eighteenth centuries," Harvard. University. Seminar on Ukrainian Studies. *Minutes*, 6 (1975-76) pp 41-44.

799. Znayenko, Myroslava T. "Tatiščev's treatment of Slavic mythology," Ph.D dissertation, Columbia University, 1973. 289 p. Available from Xerox University Microfilms.

800. Zoch, Ctiboh. "Náboženstvo pohanských Slovanov," *Orol*, 2 (1873) pp 116-7, 139-41, 162-4. (The religion of the pagan Slavs)

801. Zoll-Adamikowa, Helena. "Dei Grabsitten zwischen Elbe und Weichsel im. 6. bis 10. Jh als Quelle zur Religion der Westslawen," *Slavica Gandensia*, 7-8 (1980-81) pp 113-21.

802. Zolotov, IU. M. "O Troiane "Slove o polku Igoreve," *Sovetskaia arkheologiia*, 1970, no. 1, pp 261-3. (Concerning Troian of the Slovo o polku Igoreve)

803. Žunkovič, M. "Pripegala," *Staroslovan*, 1 (1913) H.1, pp 67-8. (Pripegala)

804. "Zur Geschichte des Religionszustandes im slavischen Mecklenburg, wie derselbe bis in das zehnte Jahrhundert gewesen," *Freimuethiges Abenblatt*, 6 (1824) no. 263, pp 33-8.

805. Żurowski, Tadeusz Roman. "Drewniany idol z Masowa," *Z otchłani wieków*, 41 (1975) no. 1, pp 20-2. (A wooden idol from Masow)

AUTHOR INDEX

SHORT TITLE INDEX

SUBJECT INDEX

OTHER BOOKS FROM SLAVICA

Ronelle Alexander: *The Structure of Vasko Popa's Poetry*, 196 p., 1986 (ISBN: 0-89357-149-0), (UCLA Slavic Studies, Volume 14).

American Contributions to the Tenth International Congress of Slavists, Sofia, September, 1988, Linguistics, edited by Alexander M. Schenker, 439 p., 1988 (ISBN: 0-89357-190-3)

American Contributions to the Tenth International Congress of Slavists, Sofia, September, 1988, Literature, edited by Jane Gary Harris, 433 p., 1988 (ISBN: 0-89357-191-1)

American Contributions to the Ninth International Congress of Slavists (Kiev 1983) *Vol. 1: Linguistics,* ed. by Michael S. Flier, 381 p., 1983 (ISBN: 0-89357-112-1).

American Contributions to the Ninth International Congress of Slavists, (Kiev 1983) *Vol. 2: Literature, Poetics, History,* ed. by Paul Debreczeny, 400 p., 1983 (ISBN: 0-89357-113-X).

American Contributions to the Eighth International Congress of Slavists (Zagreb and Ljubljana, Sept. 3-9, 1978), *Vol 1: Linguistics and Poetics,* ed. by Henrik Birnbaum, 818 p., 1978 (ISBN: 0-89357-126-1).

American Contributions to the Eighth International Congress of Slavists (Zagreb and Ljubljana, Sept. 3-9, 1978) *Vol. 2: Literature,* ed. by Victor Terras, 799 p., 1978 (ISBN: 0-89357-047-8).

Patricia M. Arant: *Russian for Reading,* 214 p., 1981 (ISBN: 0-89357-086-9).

Howard I. Aronson: *Georgian: A Reading Grammar,* 526 p., 1982 (ISBN: 0-89357-100-8).

James E. Augerot and Florin D. Popescu: *Modern Romanian,* xiv + 330 p., 1983 (ISBN: 0-89357-124-5).

Natalya Baranskaya: Неделя как неделя *Just Another Week,* edited by L. Paperno *et al.,* 92 p., 1989 (ISBN: 0-89357-202-0).

Adele Marie Barker: *The Mother Syndrome in the Russian Folk Imagination,* 180 p., 1986 (ISBN: 0-89357-160-1).

R. P. Bartlett, A. G. Cross, and Karen Rasmussen, eds.: *Russia and the World of the Eighteenth Century,* viii + 684 p., 1988 (ISBN: 0-89357-186-5).

John D. Basil: *The Mensheviks in the Revolution of 1917,* 220 p., 1984 (ISBN: 0-89357-109-1).

Henrik Birnbaum & Thomas Eekman, eds.: *Fiction and Drama in Eastern and Southeastern Europe: Evolution and Experiment in the Postwar Period,* ix + 463 p., 1980 (ISBN: 0-89357-064-8) (UCLA V. 1).

Henrik Birnbaum and Peter T. Merrill: *Recent Advances in the Reconstruction of Common Slavic (1971-1982),* vi + 141 p., 1985 (ISBN: 0-89357-116-4).

OTHER BOOKS FROM SLAVICA

Marianna D. Birnbaum: *Humanists in a Shattered World: Croatian and Hungarian Latinity in the Sixteenth Century*, 456 p., 1986 (ISBN: 0-89357-155-5). (UCLA Slavic Studies, Volume 15).

Feliks J. Bister and Herbert Kuhner, eds.: *Carinthian Slovenian Poetry*, 216 p., 1984 (ISBN: 3-85013-029-0).

Karen L. Black, ed.: *A Biobibliographical Handbook of Bulgarian Authors*, 347 p., 1982 (ISBN: 0-89357-091-5).

Marianna Bogojavlensky: *Russian Review Grammar*, xviii + 450 p., 1982 (ISBN: 0-89357-096-6).

Rodica C. Boţoman, Donald E. Corbin, E. Garrison Walters: *Îmi Place Limba Română/A Romanian Reader*, 199 p., 1982 (ISBN: 0-89357-087-7).

Richard D. Brecht and James S. Levine, eds: *Case in Slavic*, 467 p., 1986 (ISBN: 0-89357-166-0).

Gary L. Browning: *Workbook to Russian Root List*, 85 p., 1985 (ISBN: 0-89357-114-8).

Diana L. Burgin: *Richard Burgin A Life in Verse*, 230 p., 1989 (ISBN: 0-89357-196-2).

R. L. Busch: *Humor in the Major Novels of Dostoevsky*, 168 p., 1987 (ISBN: 0-89357-176-8).

Catherine V. Chvany and Richard D. Brecht, eds.: *Morphosyntax in Slavic*, v + 316 p., 1980 (ISBN: 0-89357-070-2).

Jozef Cíger-Hronský: *Jozef Mak* (a novel), translated from Slovak, 232 p., 1985 (ISBN: 0-89357-129-6).

J. Douglas Clayton, ed.: *Issues in Russian Literature Before 1917 Selected Papers of the Third World Congress for Soviet and East European Studies*, 248 p., 1989 (ISBN: 0-89357-199-7).

Frederick Columbus: *Introductory Workbook in Historical Phonology*, 39 p., 1974 (ISBN: 0-89357-018-4).

Julian W. Connolly and Sonia I. Ketchian, eds.: *Studies in Russian Literature in Honor of Vsevolod Setchkarev*, 288 p. 1987 (ISBN: 0-89357-174-1).

Gary Cox: *Tyrant and Victim in Dostoevsky*, 119 p., 1984 (ISBN: 0-89357-125-3).

Anna Lisa Crone and Catherine V. Chvany, eds.: *New Studies in Russian Language and Literature*, 302 p., 1987 (ISBN: 0-89357-168-7).

Carolina De Maegd-Soëp: *Chekhov and Women: Women in the Life and Work of Chekhov*, 373 p., 1987 (ISBN: 0-89357-175-X).

Bruce L. Derwing and Tom M. S. Priestly: *Reading Rules for Russian: A Systematic Approach to Russian Spelling and Pronunciation, with Notes on Dialectal and Stylistic Variation*, vi + 247 p., 1980 (ISBN: 0-89357-066-4).

OTHER BOOKS FROM SLAVICA

Dorothy Disterheft: *The Syntactic Development of the Infinitive in Indo-European,* 220 p., 1980 (ISBN: 0-89357-058-3).

Thomas Eekman and Dean S. Worth, eds.: *Russian Poetics* Proceedings of the International Colloquium at UCLA, September 22-26, 1975, 544 p., 1983 (ISBN: 0-89357-101-6) (UCLA Slavic Studies, Volume 4).

Mark J. Elson: *Macedonian Verbal Morphology A Structural Analysis,* 147 p., 1989 (ISBN: 0-89357-201-2).

Michael S. Flier and Richard D. Brecht, eds.: *Issues in Russian Morphosyntax,* 208 p., 1985 (ISBN: 0-89357-139-3) (UCLA V. 10).

Michael S. Flier and Alan Timberlake, eds: *The Scope of Slavic Aspect,* 295 p., 1985 (ISBN: 0-89357-150-4). (UCLA Slavic Studies 12).

John Miles Foley, ed.: *Comparative Research on Oral Traditions: A Memorial for Milman Parry,* 597 p., 1987 (ISBN: 0-89357-173-3).

John M. Foley, ed.: *Oral Traditional Literature A Festschrift for Albert Bates Lord,* 461 p., 1981 (ISBN: 0-89357-073-7).

Diana Greene: *Insidious Intent: An Interpretation of Fedor Sologub's* The Petty Demon, 140 p., 1986 (ISBN: 0-89357-158-X).

Charles E. Gribble, ed.: *Medieval Slavic Texts, Vol. 1, Old and Middle Russian Texts,* 320 p., 1973 (ISBN: 0-89357-011-7).

Charles E. Gribble: *Reading Bulgarian Through Russian,* 182 p., 1987 (ISBN: 0-89357-106-7).

Charles E. Gribble: *Russian Root List with a Sketch of Word Formation, Second Edition,* 62 p., 1982 (ISBN: 0-89357-052-4).

Charles E. Gribble: *A Short Dictionary of 18th-Century Russian*/Словарик Русского Языка 18-го Века, 103 p., 1976 (ISBN: 0-89357-172-5).

Charles E. Gribble, ed.: *Studies Presented to Professor Roman Jakobson by His Students,* 333 p., 1968, (ISBN: 0-89357-000-1).

George J. Gutsche and Lauren G. Leighton, eds.: *New Perspectives on Nineteenth-Century Russian Prose,* 146 p., 1982 (ISBN: 0-89357-094-X).

Morris Halle, ed.: *Roman Jakobson: What He Taught Us,* 94 p., 1983 (ISBN: 0-89357-118-0).

Morris Halle, Krystyna Pomorska, Elena Semeka-Pankratov, and Boris Uspenskij, eds.: *Semiotics and the History of Culture In Honor of Jurij Lotman Studies in Russian,* 437 p., 1989 (ISBN: 0-89357-195-4), (UCLA Slavic Studies, Volume 17).

Charles J. Halperin: *The Tatar Yoke,* 231 p., 1986 (ISBN: 0-89357-161-X).

William S. Hamilton: *Introduction to Russian Phonology and Word Structure,* 187 p., 1980 (ISBN: 0-89357-063-X).

Pierre R. Hart: *G. R. Derzhavin: A Poet's Progress,* iv + 164 p., 1978 (ISBN: 0-89357-054-0).

OTHER BOOKS FROM SLAVICA

Michael Heim: *Contemporary Czech*, 271 p., 1982 (ISBN: 0-89357-098-2) (UCLA Slavic Studies, Volume 3).

Michael Heim, Zlata Meyerstein, and Dean Worth: *Readings in Czech*, 147 p., 1985 (ISBN: 0-89357-154-7). (UCLA V. 13).

Warren H. Held, Jr., William R. Schmalstieg, and Janet E. Gertz: *Beginning Hittite*, ix + 218 p., 1988 (ISBN: 0-89357-184-9).

M. Hubenova & others: *A Course in Modern Bulgarian, Part 1*, viii + 303 p., 1983 (ISBN: 0-89357-104-0); *Part 2*, ix + 303 p., 1983 (ISBN: 0-89357-105-9).

Martin E. Huld: *Basic Albanian Etymologies*, x + 213 p., 1984 (ISBN: 0-89357-135-0).

Charles Isenberg: *Substantial Proofs of Being: Osip Mandelstam's Literary Prose*, 179 p., 1987 (ISBN: 0-89357-169-5).

Roman Jakobson, with the assistance of Kathy Santilli: *Brain and Language Cerebral Hemispheres and Linguistic Structure in Mutual Light*, 48 p., 1980 (ISBN: 0-89357-068-0). (New York University Slavic Papers, Interdisciplinary Series, Volume IV)

Donald K. Jarvis and Elena D. Lifshitz: *Viewpoints: A Listening and Conversation Course in Russian, Third Edition*, iv + 66 p., 1985 (ISBN: 0-89357-152-0); *Instructor's Manual*, v + 37 p., (ISBN: 0-89357-153-9).

Leslie A. Johnson: *The Experience of Time in <u>Crime and Punishment</u>*, 146 p., 1985 (ISBN: 0-89357-142-3).

Stanislav J. Kirschbaum, ed.: *East European History: Selected Papers of the Third World Congress for Soviet and East European Studies*, 183 p., 1989 (ISBN: 0-89357-193-8).

Emily R. Klenin: *Animacy in Russian: A New Interpretation*, 139 p., 1983 (ISBN: 0-89357-115-6). (UCLA Slavic Studies, Volume 6)

Andrej Kodjak, Krystyna Pomorska, and Kiril Taranovsky, eds.: *Alexander Puškin Symposium II*, 131 p., 1980 (ISBN: 0-89357-067-2) (New York University Slavic Papers, Volume III).

Andrej Kodjak, Krystyna Pomorska, Stephen Rudy, eds.: *Myth in Literature*, 207 p., 1985 (ISBN: 0-89357-137-7) (New York University Slavic Papers, Volume V).

Andrej Kodjak: *Pushkin's I. P. Belkin*, 112 p., 1979 (ISBN: 0-89357-057-5).

Andrej Kodjak, Michael J. Connolly, Krystyna Pomorska, eds.: *Structural Analysis of Narrative Texts (Conference Papers)*, 203 p., 1980 (ISBN: 0-89357-071-0) (New York University Slavic Papers, Volume II).

Demetrius J. Koubourlis, ed.: *Topics in Slavic Phonology*, vii + 270 p., 1974 (ISBN: 0-89357-017-6).

Ronald D. LeBlanc: *The Russianization of Gil Blas: A Study in Literary Appropriation*, 292 p. 1986 (ISBN: 0-89357-159-8).

Richard L. Leed, Alexander D. Nakhimovsky, and Alice S. Nakhimovsky: *Beginning Russian, Vol. 1,* xiv + 426 p., 1981 (ISBN: 0-89357-077-X); *Vol. 2,* viii + 339 p., 1982 (ISBN: 0-89357-078-8); *Teacher's Manual,* 45 p., 1981 (ISBN: 0-89357-079-6).

Richard L. Leed and Slava Paperno: *5000 Russian Words With All Their Inflected Forms: A Russian-English Dictionary,* xiv + 322 p., 1987 (ISBN: 0-89357-170-9).

Edgar H. Lehrman: *A Handbook to Eighty-Six of Chekhov's Stories in Russian,* 327 p., 1985 (ISBN: 0-89357-151-2).

Lauren Leighton, ed.: *Studies in Honor of Xenia Gąsiorowska,* 191 p., 1983 (ISBN: 0-89357-102-4).

R. L. Lencek: *The Structure and History of the Slovene Language,* 365 p., 1982 (ISBN: 0-89357-099-0).

Jules F. Levin and Peter D. Haikalis, with Anatole A. Forostenko: *Reading Modern Russian,* vi + 321 p., 1979 (ISBN: 0-89357- 059-1).

Maurice I. Levin: *Russian Declension and Conjugation:* A Structural Description with Exercises, x + 159 p., 1978 (ISBN: 0-89357-048-6).

Alexander Lipson: *A Russian Course. Part 1,* ix + 338 p., 1981 (ISBN: 0-89357-080-X); *Part 2,* 343 p., 1981 (ISBN: 0-89357-081-8); *Part 3,* iv + 105 p., 1981 (ISBN: 0-89357-082-6); *Teacher's Manual* by Stephen J. Molinsky (who also assisted in the writing of Parts 1 and 2), 222 p., 1981 (ISBN: 0-89357-083-4).

Yvonne R. Lockwood: *Text and Context Folksong in a Bosnian Muslim Village,* 220 p., 1983 (ISBN: 0-89357-120-2).

Sophia Lubensky & Donald K. Jarvis, eds.: *Teaching, Learning, Acquiring Russian,* viii + 415 p., 1984 (ISBN: 0-89357-134-2).

Horace G. Lunt: *Fundamentals of Russian,* xiv + 402 p., reprint, 1982 (ISBN: 0-89357-097-4).

Paul Macura: *Russian-English Botanical Dictionary,* 678 p., 1982 (ISBN: 0-89357-092-3).

Thomas G. Magner, ed.: *Slavic Linguistics and Language Teaching,* x + 309 p., 1976 (ISBN: 0-89357-037-0).

Amy Mandelker and Roberta Reeder, eds.: *The Supernatural in Slavic and Baltic Literature: Essays in Honor of Victor Terras,* Introduction by J. Thomas Shaw, xxi + 402 p., 1989 (ISBN: 0-89357-192-X).

Vladimir Markov and Dean S. Worth, eds.: *From Los Angeles to Kiev Papers on the Occasion of the Ninth International Congress of Slavists,* 250 p., 1983 (ISBN: 0-89357-119-9) (UCLA Slavic Studies, Volume 7).

Mateja Matejić and Dragan Milivojević: *An Anthology of Medieval Serbian Literature in English,* 205 p., 1978 (ISBN: 0-89357-055-9).

OTHER BOOKS FROM SLAVICA

Peter J. Mayo: *The Morphology of Aspect in Seventeenth-Century Russian (Based on Texts of the Smutnoe Vremja)*, xi + 234 p., 1985 (ISBN: 0-89357-145-8).

Arnold McMillin, ed.: *Aspects of Modern Russian and Czech Literature Selected Papers of the Third World Congress for Soviet and East European Studies*, 239 p., 1989 (ISBN: 0-89357-194-6).

Gordon M. Messing: *A Glossary of Greek Romany As Spoken in Agia Varvara (Athens)*, 175 p., 1988 (ISBN: 0-89357-187-3).

Vasa D. Mihailovich and Mateja Matejic: *A Comprehensive Bibliography of Yugoslav Literature in English, 1593-1980*, xii + 586 p., 1984 (ISBN: 0-89357-136-9).

Vasa D. Mihailovich: *First Supplement to A Comprehensive Bibliography of Yugoslav Literature in English 1981-1985*, 338 p., 1989 (ISBN: 0-89357-188-1).

Edward Mozejko, ed.: *Vasiliy Pavlovich Aksenov: A Writer in Quest of Himself*, 272 p., 1986 (ISBN: 0-89357-141-5).

Edward Możejko: *Yordan Yovkov*, 117 p., 1984 (ISBN: 0-89357-117-2).

Alexander D. Nakhimovsky and Richard L. Leed: *Advanced Russian, Second Edition, Revised*, vii + 262 p., 1987 (ISBN: 0-89357-178-4).

The Comprehensive Russian Grammar of A. A. Barsov/ Обстоятельная грамматика А. А. Барсова, Critical Edition by Lawrence W. Newman, lxxxvi + 382 p., 1980 (ISBN: 0-89357-072-9).

Felix J. Oinas: *Essays on Russian Folklore and Mythology*, 183 p., 1985, (ISBN: 0-89357-148-2).

Hongor Oulanoff: *The Prose Fiction of Veniamin Kaverin*, v + 203 p., 1976 (ISBN: 0-89357-032-X).

Temira Pachmuss: *Russian Literature in the Baltic between the World Wars*, 448 p., 1988 (ISBN: 0-89357-181-4).

Lora Paperno: *Getting Around Town in Russian: Situational Dialogs*, English translation and photographs by Richard D. Sylvester, 123 p., 1987 (ISBN: 0-89357-171-7).

Slava Paperno, Alexander D. Nakhimovsky, Alice S. Nakhimovsky, and Richard L. Leed: *Intermediate Russian: The Twelve Chairs*, 326 p., 1985, (ISBN: 0-89357-144-X).

Ruth L. Pearce: *Russian For Expository Prose, Vol. 1 Introductory Course*, 413 p., 1983 (ISBN: 0-89357-121-0); *Vol. 2 Advanced Course*, 255 p., 1983 (ISBN: 0-89357-122-9).

Jan L. Perkowski: *The Darkling A Treatise on Slavic Vampirism*, 169 p., 1989 (ISBN: 0-89357-200-4).

Gerald Pirog: *Aleksandr Blok's Итальянские Стихи Confrontation and Disillusionment*, 219 p., 1983 (ISBN: 0-89357-095-8).

OTHER BOOKS FROM SLAVICA

Stanley J. Rabinowitz: *Sologub's Literary Children: Keys to a Symbolist's Prose*, 176 p., 1980 (ISBN: 0-89357-069-9).

Gilbert C. Rappaport: *Grammatical Function and Syntactic Structure: The Adverbial Participle of Russian*, 218 p., 1984 (ISBN: 0-89357-133-4) (UCLA Slavic Studies, Volume 9).

David F. Robinson: *Lithuanian Reverse Dictionary*, ix + 209 p., 1976 (ISBN: 0-89357-034-6).

Don K. Rowney & G. Edward Orchard, eds.: *Russian and Slavic History*, viii + 303 p., 1977 (ISBN: 0-89357-036-2).

Catherine Rudin: *Aspects of Bulgarian Syntax: Complementizers and WH Constructions*, iv + 232 p., 1986, (ISBN: 0-89357-156-3).

Gerald J. Sabo, S.J., ed.: *Valaská Škola, by Hugolin Gavlovič, with a linguistic sketch by Ľ. Ďurovič, 730 p., 1988* (ISBN: 0-89357-179-2).

Ernest A. Scatton: *Bulgarian Phonology*, xii + 224 p., 1975 (reprint: 1983) (ISBN: 0-89357-103-2).

Ernest A. Scatton: *A Reference Grammar of Modern Bulgarian*, 448 p., 1984 (ISBN: 0-89357-123-7).

Barry P. Scherr and Dean S. Worth, eds.: *Russian Verse Theory Proceedings of the 1987 Conference at UCLA*, 514 p., 1989 (ISBN: 0-89357-198-9).

William R. Schmalstieg: *Introduction to Old Church Slavic, second edition*, 314 p., 1983 (ISBN: 0-89357-107-5).

William R. Schmalstieg: *A Lithuanian Historical Syntax*, xi + 412 p., 1988 (ISBN: 0-89357-185-7).

R. D. Schupbach: *Lexical Specialization in Russian*, 102 p., 1984 (ISBN: 0-89357-128-8) (UCLA Slavic Studies, Volume 8).

Peter Seyffert: *Soviet Literary Structuralism: Background Debate Issues*, 378 p., 1985 (ISBN: 0-89357-140-7).

Kot K. Shangriladze and Erica W. Townsend, eds.: *Papers for the V. Congress of Southeast European Studies (Belgrade, September 1984)*, 382 p., 1984 (ISBN: 0-89357-138-5).

Michael Shapiro: *Aspects of Russian Morphology, A Semiotic Investigation*, 62 p. (7 x 10" format), 1969 (ISBN: 0-89357-004-4).

J. Thomas Shaw: *Pushkin A Concordance to the Poetry*, 2 volumes, 1310 pages total, 1985 (ISBN: 0-89357-130-X for the set).

Efraim Sicher: *Style and Structure in the Prose of Isaak Babel'*, 169 p., 1986 (ISBN: 0-89357-163-6).

Mark S. Simpson: *The Russian Gothic Novel and its British Antecedents*, 112 p., 1986 (ISBN: 0-89357-162-8).

David A. Sloane: *Aleksandr Blok and the Dynamics of the Lyric Cycle*, 384 p., 1988 (ISBN: 0-89357-182-2).

OTHER BOOKS FROM SLAVICA

Greta N. Slobin, ed.: *Aleksej Remizov: Approaches to a Protean Writer*, 286 p., 1987 (ISBN: 0-89357-167-9).

Theofanis G. Stavrou and Peter R. Weisensel: *Russian Travelers to the Christian East from the Twelfth to the Twentieth Century*, L + 925 p., 1985, (ISBN: 0-89357-157-1).

Gerald Stone and Dean S. Worth, eds.: *The Formation of the Slavonic Literary Languages, Proceedings of a Conference Held in Memory of Robert Auty and Anne Pennington at Oxford 6-11 July 1981*, 269 p., 1985 (ISBN: 0-89357-143-1) (UCLA Slavic Studies, Volume 11).

Roland Sussex and J. C. Eade, eds.: *Culture and Nationalism in Nineteenth-Century Eastern Europe*, 158 p., 1985 (ISBN: 0-89357-146-6).

Oscar E. Swan: *First Year Polish, second edition, revised and expanded*, 354 p., 1983 (ISBN: 0-89357-108-3).

Oscar E. Swan: *Intermediate Polish*, 370 p., 1986 (ISBN: 0-89357-165-2).

Jane A. Taubman: *A Life Through Verse Marina Tsvetaeva's Lyric Diary*, 296 p., 1989 (ISBN: 0-89357-197-0).

Charles E. Townsend: *Continuing With Russian*, xxi + 426 p., 1981 (ISBN: 0-89357-085-0).

Charles E. Townsend and Veronica N. Dolenko: *Instructor's Manual to Accompany Continuing With Russian*, 39 p., 1987 (ISBN: 0-89357-177-6).

Charles E. Townsend: *Czech Through Russian*, viii + 263 p., 1981 (ISBN: 0-89357-089-3).

Charles E. Townsend: *The Memoirs of Princess Natal'ja Borisovna Dolgorukaja*, viii + 146 p., 1977 (ISBN: 0-89357-044-3).

Charles E. Townsend: *Russian Word Formation, corrected reprint*, viii + 272 p., 1975 (ISBN: 0-89357-023-0).

Janet G. Tucker: *Innokentij Annenskij and the Acmeist Doctrine*, 154 p., 1987 (ISBN: 0-89357-164-4).

Boryana Velcheva: *Proto-Slavic and Old Bulgarian Sound Changes*, Translation of the original by Ernest A. Scatton, 187 p., 1988 (ISBN: 0-89357-189-X).

Walter N. Vickery, ed.: *Aleksandr Blok Centennial Conference*, 403 p., 1984, (ISBN: 0-89357-111-3).

Essays in Honor of A. A. Zimin, ed. D. C. Waugh, xiv + 416 p., 1985 (ISBN: 0-89357-147-4).

Daniel C. Waugh: *The Great Turkes Defiance On the History of the Apocryphal Correspondence of the Ottoman Sultan in its Muscovite and Russian Variants*, ix + 354 p., 1978 (ISBN: 0-89357-056-7).

Susan Wobst: *Russian Readings and Grammatical Terminology*, 88 p., 1978 (ISBN: 0-89357-049-4).

OTHER BOOKS FROM SLAVICA

James B. Woodward: *The Symbolic Art of Gogol: Essays on His Short Fiction,* 131 p., 1982 (ISBN: 0-89357-093-1).

Dean S. Worth: *Origins of Russian Grammar Notes on the state of Russian philology before the advent of printed grammars,* 176 p., 1983 (ISBN 0-89357-110-5). (UCLA Slavic Studies, Volume 5)

Что я видел *What I Saw* by Boris Zhitkov, Annotated and Edited by Richard L. Leed and Lora Paperno, 128 p. (8.5 x 11" format), 1988 (ISBN: 0-89357-183-0).